H. S Thompson

Ireland in 1839 and 1869

H. S Thompson

Ireland in 1839 and 1869

ISBN/EAN: 9783337323868

Printed in Europe, USA, Canada, Australia, Japan

Cover: Foto ©ninafisch / pixelio.de

More available books at **www.hansebooks.com**

IRELAND

IN

1839 AND 1869.

BY H. S. THOMPSON,

LATE PRESIDENT OF THE
ROYAL AGRICULTURAL SOCIETY OF ENGLAND.

LONDON:
DORRELL AND SON, CHARING CROSS.
DUBLIN: HODGES, FOSTER, AND CO.
1870.

CONTENTS.

	PAGE
INTRODUCTION	1
TESTS OF NATIONAL PROGRESS	3
Increase of Wealth	4
Improved Condition of Labouring Classes	10
Agricultural Improvement	14
Pauperism and the Poor Law	42
Rents and Farmers' Profits	46
LAND TENURE	52
Fixity of Tenure	53
Compulsory Leases	67
Tenancy-at-Will	68
Long Leases	83
ULSTER TENANT-RIGHT	87
SUMMARY OF SUGGESTIONS	107

IRELAND IN 1839 AND 1869.

"O, wad some Pow'r the giftie gie us,
To see oursels as others see us."—*Burns*.

IT is announced on authority that the Irish Land Question will be taken up in the approaching Session of Parliament. In Ireland, where this question ought to be well understood, many modes of dealing with it have been proposed, and the advocates of each plan believe all others to be impracticable. The educated classes in England will, therefore, have to act as arbitrators in this matter; and to ensure their being thoroughly well informed on the subject before they are called upon to give a decision, facts and opinions should be contributed from every quarter.

The writer of these pages having, in 1839, spent some months in Ireland endeavouring to make himself acquainted with the peculiar usage known by the name of *Ulster Tenant Right*, and with the condition of the peasant population in the southern and western counties, it occurred to him that by repeating his visit after thirty years' absence, he would be enabled to place before the public a comparative view of the state of Ireland in 1839 and 1869, which might throw some light upon the important questions connected with Land Tenure. Acting upon this conviction, he has devoted the last few months to visiting the sister country, and having been kindly furnished with letters of introduction to men of all classes, creeds, and political opinions, he put himself freely into communication with both landlords and tenants, consulted the clergy as well as the laity, exchanged ideas with men of all professions and no profession, and, in short, neglected no opportunity of collecting information and ascertaining the opinions of Irishmen on the present anomalies of their social system.

In the course of his tour, he passed through every county in Ireland, and personally visited estates, the aggregate extent of which considerably exceeded one million and a half of statute acres. In all cases he was accompanied either by the owner, the resident agent, or the occupier of the land, in some instances by all three, which enabled him to ascertain on the best authority the acreage, rent, and other particulars.

He takes this early opportunity of expressing his deep sense of the kind and hospitable reception experienced during the whole of his tour. From the Lord-Lieutenant downwards through all ranks and classes of society, he received the utmost courtesy and attention, and found every one willing to impart information and to further the object he had in view. Whilst tendering his cordial thanks, he cannot forbear from also congratulating the nation that the graceful hospitality and courteous demeanour towards strangers for which they have long been noted, should have preserved all their former freshness through the heats of party strife and the bitterness of religious differences. It holds out fair promise for the future, by showing that the warm hearted generosity of the Irish character is in no wise diminished, and that if the right vein be but struck, Englishmen will accomplish the object they so much desire, viz., a practical repeal of the present union between the two countries, by substituting for it a union of hearts and hands founded on mutual respect and esteem.

National Progress.

When considering the expediency of suggested legislative changes, especially such as would directly affect large masses of property, and modify the existing relations between important classes of society, it is desirable to ascertain, in the first instance, whether the country whose laws it is proposed to alter is in an improving, a stationary, or a declining condition. For it is obvious that a measure which is designed merely to assist and accelerate a rate of advance already established, must differ in its leading features from one which is calculated to arrest a course of progressive decline, and develop new sources of national prosperity.

A journey of some thousand miles through the various counties of Ireland has made it impossible for the writer to doubt, that in the last thirty years there has been generally throughout the country, a great development of all the elements of national prosperity. *Wealth has increased, the condition of the labouring classes has materially improved, and the progress of agriculture, with certain exceptions, has been highly satisfactory.*

Wealth has increased.—If increased means may fairly be inferred from increased expenditure, no doubt can be entertained of the fact that the wealth of the upper and middle classes in Ireland has of late years largely increased, and is now steadily increasing. A visit to the sea-bathing places along the east coast, from Belfast Lough in the North, to Wexford in the extreme South, would satisfy the most sceptical that unless the professional and trading classes in the towns were thriving, new villas and lodging-houses would not be springing up wherever the lovely scenery of that coast could be seen to most advantage. This is by no means confined to the East coast. Cork, Limerick, and even Galway, which has had much to contend with, from the nearly total loss of its herring-fishery, can all boast of their villas and their sea-bathing places, the beauty of whose position and scenery could scarcely be surpassed. It is unnecessary to go round the island, but Sligo must not be omitted, as one of the principal of the coast towns, which provide lodging-houses, of very moderate pretensions, for the accommodation of the humbler classes, when they, to use the phrase of the country, "go to the *salt water*," and no one can witness without pleasure, the joyous migration of crowds of the lower middle classes to and from these little marine residences.

The great improvement in the character of the private dwellings throughout Ireland since 1841 is well shown in the Report of the Census Commissioners of 1861, which gives the relative numbers of inhabited houses in Ireland in 1841 and 1861 divided into four classes:—

TOTAL NUMBER OF INHABITED HOUSES—IRELAND.*

	1841.	1861.	Increase.	Decrease.
1st Class	40,080	55,416	15,336	
2nd Do.	264,184	360,698	96,514	
3rd Do.	533,297	489,668	..	43,629
4th Do.	491,278	89,374	..	401,904

The Commissioners of 1841 state "That in the lowest or 4th class were comprised all mud cabins having only one room." Whatever opinion may be entertained of the national advantage or disadvantage of the great decrease of 2,397,630 in the population of Ireland between 1841 and 1861, it is highly satisfactory to find that the consequent decrease in the number of inhabited houses has been entirely confined to the 3rd and 4th classes, which show a falling off of 445,533, of which 43,629, or less than one-tenth were in the 3rd class, and the remaining

---

* Census (1861), Part V. p. xix.

nine-tenths in the fourth or lowest class of human
habitations. It also appears that in the same period
there has been an increase of 15,336 in the number
of 1st-class houses, and of 96,514 in those of the
2nd class. An absolute increase of 111,850 first
and second class houses in twenty years, or on the
average 5592 yearly, affords conclusive proof of
the rapid increase of the middle classes in Ireland
during the period in question both in wealth and
numbers.

The evidences of increasing wealth are, however,
by no means confined to the sea coast, or to private residences. In all the principal towns public
buildings of a substantial and handsome appearance
have been erected since 1839. New churches, banks,
asylums, are everywhere to be met with, and English
magistrates and guardians of the poor might with
advantage visit the Irish court-houses and union
workhouses. The ornamental character of these
buildings is doubtless partly due to the beauty of
the blue limestone of which they are for the most
part built, but their designs show good taste, as
well as fitness for their purpose, and the sites
have in general been selected with great judgment,
so that they contrast very favourably with the
barrack-like appearance of many public buildings in
England. When it is borne in mind that the whole
of the workhouses (there are in Ireland 163 Poor
Law Unions), and a large proportion of the other
public buildings have been erected since 1839, and

that in the same time 28 millions sterling have been expended in the construction of railways, it must be admitted that the country has rapidly advanced in the outward and visible signs of material prosperity.

Improvement in the public and private buildings of a country is probably the most certain indication of the increase of national wealth, but the condition of its trade is scarcely less significant, and in this respect also the records of the last thirty years prove that Ireland has advanced with no doubtful or halting steps. The increase of business and shipping at the principal ports attracts the notice of all visitors, and the following extract from the Report of the Dublin Port and Docks Board for the year ending Dec. 31, 1868, shows the extent of the progress made at that port. It should be mentioned that the Board contemplate extensive works for the enlargement and improvement of the Port, and in support of these measures state that " In the last thirty years shipping engaged in the foreign or over-sea trade has increased *fourfold*, steam coasters *threefold*, and sailing coasting-vessels, including colliers, *seventy* per cent." The total registered tonnage of shipping that entered the Port of Dublin being in

1838	=	581,183
1868	=	1,420,292

| Increase in 30 years | 839,109 | = | 144 per cent. |

				Tons of Shipping.
Average of 10 years	..	1839—1848	=	639,111
Ditto ditto	..	1849—1858	=	869,523
Ditto ditto	..	1859—1868	=	1,231,526

In another part of the Report, it is stated that in 1868 "The aggregate tonnage of vessels entering the Port was rather less than in 1867, the decrease has, however, not amounted to one per cent." The whole decrease of tonnage in 1868 was 13,730, and of dues 100*l.*, when compared with the preceding year; but this trifling decline has been far more than made up in 1869, the returns for the first eleven months showing an increase in the tonnage of 84,598, and in the dues of 6419*l.*, over the corresponding eleven months of 1868.

The trade of Belfast has increased equally rapidly; the tonnage of shipping entering that port being in

1846	=	543,862	
1868	=	1,201,306	
Increase in 22 years		657,444	= 120 per cent.

These returns prove in the most unexceptionable way the rapid development of the internal resources of the country, as that alone could maintain so great and continuous an advance in both the coasting and foreign trade through such a number of years.

In any estimate of national wealth Bank deposits and private balances must always form a prominent item. Dr. Neilson Hancock was the first to point out its special bearing on the present inquiry in his able report to the Irish Government in 1863.[*] In p. 50 of that Report, referring to the "Deposits in

---

[*] 'Report on the supposed progressive Decline of Irish Prosperity. By W. Neilson Hancock, LL.D.'

Joint-Stock Banks," he says "It is a test which derives considerable importance from the fact that the farmers are understood to be the most numerous class of depositors." In the same Report Dr. Hancock published a table showing the increase and decrease of the Bank deposits from 1840 to 1862. Mr. Thom, the well-known Dublin publisher, has kindly supplied the materials for continuing that return to the present time.

TABLE showing the aggregate amount of the PRIVATE BALANCES in the BANK OF IRELAND, and of the DEPOSITS in the several JOINT-STOCK BANKS in IRELAND at the 31st December, from 1863 to 1866 inclusive, and at the 30th of June from 1867 to 1869 inclusive—

	£.		£.
1863	12,996,731	1867	19,211,342
1864	14,442,176	1868	18,437,128
1865	17,050,552	1869	19,665,443
1866	18,975,046		

Dr. Hancock gives an elaborate explanation of the causes of the considerable fluctuations in the Bank deposits, which are shown in his table to have occurred in different years. That table, which is too long for insertion here, proves that notwithstanding the occasional decline caused by a monetary crisis or by bad harvests, there is on the whole a steadily advancing current of progress which has continued to the present time and has raised these deposits from 5,567,851*l*. in 1840 to 19,665,443*l*. in 1869. The following table gives the average amount of private balances in the Bank of Ireland, and of deposits in the Joint-Stock Banks during three successive periods of ten years each—

		£.
1840—1849	=	7,008,141
1850—1859	=	12,021,151
1860—1869	=	16,578,144

Hence it appears that if the inquiry be extended over a sufficient number of years to prevent the influence of a very good or very bad season from being unduly felt, the Bank deposits show, like the shipping, a continuous increase which can scarcely be explained on any other supposition than a steady augmentation of national wealth.

Improvement in the Condition of the Labouring Classes.—In every county questions were put to the employers of labour as to the actual rate now paid as compared with the wages earned thirty years ago. Almost without exception it was stated that wages had doubled during that interval, and that a great improvement had taken place in the labourers' diet; those in regular employment, especially in the towns, being large consumers of wheaten bread, an article of diet which, a quarter of a century ago, was completely out of the reach of any working man. Even the ordinary farm labourers are not limited, as formerly, to the potato; Indian-meal being largely used by them, especially when potatoes are dear, or when they begin to lose their goodness, in the later months of spring. It was asserted, on good medical authority, that this higher standard, and greater variety of diet, had diminished greatly a distressing class of cases which formerly prevailed extensively in the early summer months, commencing with flatulence and dyspepsia, and ending in dysentery and fever, thus incapacitating the labourer from work, at a time of year when his labour was most valuable to him. The increased use of shoes and stockings, and the general improvement in the dress and appearance of the servants and labouring classes, are too evident to require proof.

Another satisfactory indication of progress is afforded by the great diminution in the number of destitute and unoccupied persons. *Where are the beggars?* was a question continually suggesting itself. Formerly all places of public resort were beset by the most painful evidences of the number and variety of the ills to which human nature is subject. The Poor Law must have the credit of having provided an asylum for these unfortunates; and though union workhouses may not be desirable residences, it is a clear gain to all parties, that those on whom the hand of affliction presses so heavily, should not be compelled to earn a precarious livelihood by parading their misery before the public eye, and that they should always be assured of food and shelter in comparative quiet and retirement.

It is equally gratifying to see how much the *loiterers* are reduced in number. Thirty years ago it was usual, in even the smallest town, to see parties of able-bodied men idling in the market-place because no man had hired them. It is still so in some few parts of the country, but the extent to which the idlers have been reduced may be inferred from the fact that the regular daily work of the country has largely increased, whilst the number of the population has been reduced by more than two millions and a half, and one of the most hopeful signs for the future, is to be found in the greater *variety* of work now obtainable. There has been no sudden change of occupation, but gradually, as wealth has increased, more men have been required to supply the wants of a nation advancing in civilization. The building trades especially have employed more hands, manufactures have been quietly extending, railways have required clerks, porters, and plate-layers, and when summed up into a total it is found that, whilst in 1841 66·1 out of every 100 families in Ireland were engaged in agriculture, in 1861 only 42·6 per cent. were so employed.* In 1841, when the population reached 8,196,597, two-thirds of the people were supported by agriculture. In 1861, when the population had fallen to 5,798,967, only 42½ per cent. of that reduced number were dependent on the land. .

It might be supposed that this change of occupation on the part of so large a portion of the people was due to a diminution of agricultural employment caused by the increase of grass, and diminution of arable farming, but on referring to the official returns this is not found to be the case—

---

* Census (1861), Part V. p. xxiii.

TOTAL OF IRELAND.*

	Arable Land.	Plantations.	Towns.	Water.	Uncultivated.
	Acres.	Acres.	Acres.	Acres.	Acres.
1841	13,464,300	374,482	42,929	630,825	6,295,735
1851	14,802,581	304,906	45,590	631,210	5,023,984
1861	15,464,825	316,597	49,236	627,464	4,357,338

It appears from this table that between 1841 and 1861 the "arable land" (which in this return includes grass land) had increased from 13,464,300 to 15,464,825 statute acres, and the uncultivated land had decreased to nearly the same extent, viz., from 6,295,735 to 4,357,338 statute acres. The statistics furnished by the Registrar-General show further that in 1847 (the earliest date at which the acreage of crops was published separately) the total acreage under crops was 5,238,575, and in 1861 was 5,890,536 acres, showing an increase of 651,961 acres; and though the corn crops had decreased by 688,622 acres, the increase in green crops was 843,678 acres, in flax 89,645 acres, and in meadow and clover 407,260 acres. To any one acquainted with farming it is scarcely necessary to point out that the increased area of green crops, flax, meadow and clover (chiefly for hay), amounting to 1,340,583 acres, would furnish far more work for the labourer than the 688,622 acres of corn for which these green crops were partially substituted.

* Census (1861), Part V. p. viii.

A large area of land has undoubtedly been laid down to permanent grass since the famine years, but a sufficient quantity of previously uncultivated land has been reclaimed to prevent any diminution in the agricultural employment of the people. *Additional work*, has also been created by the great increase of green crops consequent upon the spread of improved farming. And this increased work was done in 1861 by 42½ per cent. of a greatly reduced population, whereas the smaller work of 1841 was nominally performed by 66·1 per cent. of a population of eight millions, thus showing how large a proportion of those eight millions could only have been partially employed, and at the current rate of remuneration very insufficiently maintained by those agricultural pursuits to which alone they devoted their lives.

The three tests of national progress proposed for consideration were, *Increase of wealth, improvement in the condition of the labouring classes*, and a satisfactory *rate of advance in practical agriculture*, of which the last still remains to be dealt with.

Agricultural Improvement.—In order to form a sound opinion respecting the state and prospects of Irish farming, it is necessary to look first at the general outline of the country, which is very peculiar, the coast as a rule being composed of high mountains and the interior for the most part being flat. Clouds highly charged with moisture from the ocean meeting these mountain ranges discharge excessive quantities of rain, of which the greater part runs inland, and making its way slowly across extensive plains forms that succession of inland lakes and streams which adds much to the beauty of the landscape, but unfortunately much also to the difficulties of the husbandman. Wherever, from the prostration of ancient forests or other causes, the watercourses have been obstructed, whole districts have gradually been converted into bogs. A large rainfall, extensive sheets of water very liable in wet seasons to overflow the adjoining lands, and a level country interspersed with bogs, frequently of large area, all point to the same conclusion, viz., that arterial drainage is an essential preliminary to the proper cultivation of a considerable portion of the country.

The difficulties of main drainage in a level country are in Ireland greatly enhanced by the smallness of the holdings, and the intense sensitiveness of the occupiers to any apparent encroachment or interference with their land. No main-drainage scheme, therefore, of any extent could be carried into effect until the appointment of the present Board of Public Works, with parliamentary powers, about the year 1830. In the 37th Report of the Commissioners (published 1869), it is stated that since the formation of the board 266,736 acres of flooded or injured lands have been drained or improved, the cost of which, including interest, has been 8*l.* 11*s.* 4*d.* per acre, and the "*increase in the annual letting value of these lands caused by drainage*" 74,502*l.* The expenditure, therefore, of about two millions and a quarter has produced an increase of rent equal to 3¼ per cent. on the money laid out. Looking at it in a national point of view this rate of interest may fairly be doubled, as tenants would not give that additional rent unless they saw their way to at least an equal amount of profit; so that, besides the health and comfort derived from these works by the inhabitants of the districts where they are carried on, the addition thus made to the national resources may be considered equivalent to interest at the rate of 6 or 7 per cent. on the money advanced. Works of this character are still greatly needed, and as the repayments are regularly made, it is much to be hoped that these advances will be more largely made use of. It is satisfactory to learn that in the years 1868-9 the works have been proceeding at a more rapid rate than for several previous years, but it was pointed out by the officers of the board that applications are considerably checked by the great delay which occurs before a grant can be obtained in consequence of the necessity of application being made for parliamentary sanction to each individual scheme.

Of the three most characteristic features of the country, the coast ranges of mountains and the bogs have already been alluded to; the third is the great gravel drift which overspreads a large portion of the land, and gives a decided tone to its agriculture. It varies much in its nature from a pure shingle to a strong clayey gravel, but generally abounds in pebbles and boulders of the carboniferous limestone. The natural tendency of the soil wherever this drift extends is to run to grass: in some districts it forms excellent grazing land, technically said to fatten "two crops a year," in other counties it is admirable for dairy purposes, and the lighter portion of the drift is very suitable for sheep, and would be called in England good turnip and barley land.

The great prevalence of limestone gravel, and the mildness and humidity of the climate, make "laying down land to grass" a simple and natural process in Ireland, although so tedious and expensive an operation in most parts of England. Unfortunately this valuable facility has been made the foundation of a somewhat exhaustive system of husbandry. The Irish four-course shift is: 1. Potatoes or turnips. 2. Oats, barley, or wheat. 3. Grass. 4. Oats. This is frequently extended to a six-years' course by allowing the grass to remain another year, in which case it is mown the first year and pastured the next. After this, two crops of oats are generally taken. The average length of a rotation of crops in Ireland may therefore be assumed to be five years. Such a course of husbandry, whether limited to four, or extended over the longer period of six years, contains an equal number of exhausting and restorative crops, but loses a large portion of the restorative effect in consequence of the potatoes, and even the turnips (where turnips are grown), being entirely removed from the land, and the grass or clover being mown for hay. On land of good body this course may not be injurious, but a large portion of Ireland is very light in staple, and nothing but green crops consumed on the land by sheep can give it the requisite richness and solidity for bearing heavy crops of grain. The tendency now is to lay down this description of land to permanent grass, in consequence of the rise in wages and in the value of cattle and dairy produce. This is doubtful policy. There are extensive districts in some of the Midland and South-Eastern counties which are eminently suited for convertible husbandry, and would produce good crops of corn; but this land, when in grass, carries very little stock, and to make it really profitable would require frequent top-dressing. This, it need hardly be said, is rarely done, the systematic top-dressing of pastures being the latest development of the most advanced farming in England.

But, it will be asked, if this be the present state of Irish agriculture, in what is the great improvement to be seen? Those who were conversant with Irish agriculture thirty years ago will be at no loss to answer this question. The *prevalent* system then was precisely what is to be seen now in those exceptional districts where no improvement has taken place. It would be invidious to point out individual farms or estates, but no one can travel far in Ireland, especially in the western counties, without passing through places where the population is still redundant and miserable, and the holdings so small that no regular course of husbandry could be adopted, even if the occupiers possessed the requisite knowledge and capital.

The common practice on these holdings, and unfortunately on some others where better things are possible, is to grow potatoes once or twice, then oats as long as possible. Cases of *eight or ten crops in succession, without manure,* are occasionally met with. After that the land is, to use their own expression, "*laid to waste*" without sowing clover or grass of any kind, and it is left in this state overrun with weeds until the natural tendency of this grass country gradually produces a sort of rough sward, when it is again ploughed out, and a crop or two of corn taken, or the potato course recommenced; for in farming of this kind nothing like a regular system is attempted, the acreage of potatoes grown depending entirely on the quantity of manure at command, and the extent sown with corn being in like manner limited only by the capability of the land to produce anything more than will pay for seed and labour.

The following Table, consisting of Extracts from the Government returns, shows the total acreage under crops in 1869 and in 1847, the earliest date at which the acreage of crops was published separately;

	1847.	1869.	Decrease.	Increase.
	Acres.	Acres.	Acres.	Acres.
Corn crops	3,313,579	2,207,970	1,105,609	
Green crops	727,738	1,468,895	..	741,157
Meadow and clover	1,138,946	1,669,800	..	530,854
Flax	58,312	229,178	..	170,866
Total acreage under crops	5,238,575	5,575,843	..	337,268

It appears that in 1869 there were 337,268 acres more under crop than in 1847; that the corn-crops had decreased to the extent of 1,105,609 acres, whilst the green crops had increased 741,157, the meadow and clover 530,854, and the flax 170,866 acres respectively; thus furnishing incontrovertible proof that great progress had been made in those twenty-two years in sowing land down to clover and grass, instead of leaving it to waste, and in substituting the growth of green crops for the exhaustive and unprofitable succession of corn-crops previously in vogue. The Government returns, when examined in detail, also show that the change is not confined to any particular district, but, on the contrary, so generally distributed over the country as to deserve the name of "*National Progress.*"

The agricultural improvement is not, however, confined to the spread of a better course of husbandry. The increase in live-stock is also very striking, and admits of direct proof. Comparing the returns given by the Registrar-General, for the first and last years for which these statistics are furnished, we find that the number of cattle, sheep, and pigs, in these years, were as follow:—

	1841.	1869.	Increase or Decrease of Number.	Increase or decrease of value at Census Comrs. Rates (1841).
Cattle	1,863,166	3,727,794	Increase. 1,864,628	Increase. £12,120,082
Sheep	2,106,189	4,648,158	2,541,969	2,796,165
Pigs	1,412,813	1,079,793	Decrease. 333,020	Decrease. 416,275

The number of cattle and sheep had therefore doubled, and their value had increased in these twenty-eight years by nearly fifteen millions sterling, at the rates fixed by the Census Commissioners of 1841, and since retained as the official standard of value—viz., 6*l.* 10*s.* per head for cattle, 1*l.* 2*s.* for sheep, and 1*l.* 5*s.* for pigs. These rates are much below the present worth of the animals, their weight and quality having within the last thirty years been much increased by the greater attention paid to their breeding and feeding. The market price of all descriptions of live-stock has also materially advanced in the same period. In Thom's invaluable Official Almanac (1868), an estimate is given of the increased value, which fixes the rates at 8*l.* 18*s.* per head for cattle, 1*l.* 17*s.* for sheep, and 2*l.* 18*s.* for pigs. This seems a moderate estimate, and, applying it to the numbers of live-stock given above, the increased value between 1841 and 1869 would be:—Cattle, 16,595,190*l.*; sheep,

4,702,644*l.*; pigs (decrease), 965,758*l.* : total increase, 20,332,076*l.*

The diminution in the number of pigs has been much commented upon, as showing a serious decline in the poor man's stock. It has also been supposed to be connected with the great decline in the numbers of the population. This is an error. A rapid rise or fall in the number and price of pigs is familiar to farmers in other countries as well as Ireland, and the reasons are obvious. A farmer can increase his stock of pigs in a few months, and he is guided in the number which he rears in any particular season chiefly by the price of grain and the productiveness of the potato-crop. When grain is dear, it pays the producer better to sell his corn in the market; when it is cheap, he can frequently make more of it by converting it into pork. That the recent decline in the number of pigs is due to this cause is apparent on looking at the return of the total number of pigs in Ireland for some years back :—

Year		Pigs	Year		Pigs
1858	..	1,409,883	1864	..	1,058,480
1859	..	1,265,751	1865	..	1,305,953
1860	..	1,271,072	1866	..	1,497,274
1861	..	1,102,042	1867	..	1,235,191
1862	..	1,154,324	1868	..	869,578
1863	..	1,067,458	1869	..	1,079,793

In 1858 the number of pigs was the highest arrived at from the commencement of the publication of these statistics. From this time the numbers fell off, until, in 1864, they were only 1,058,480; and a decline extending, with scarcely any interruption, over six years might easily have been attributed to the marvellous emigration which, in the fourteen years 1850-1864, had removed a million and a half of souls from the shores of Ireland. But *after* this great diminution of population, and when the stream of emigration was rapidly declining, the number of pigs, in 1865, *increased by a quarter of a million!* and, in 1866, by a further 191,000, thus reaching the previously unexampled number of 1,497,274. The high price of corn and meal in 1868 again reduced the number to the very low figure of 869,578; but they have increased again in 1869, and will doubtless continue to fluctuate accordingly as the price of pig-food is high enough or low enough to make the rearing and fattening of pigs a profitable or a losing speculation. After allowing for the decrease in the number and value of the pigs in 1869, when compared with 1841, the Live-Stock Statistics for those years show that the cattle and sheep have more than *doubled in number;* and the value of the cattle, sheep, and pigs, together, has increased by more than twenty millions sterling!

Another branch of improvement, in which agriculture in Ireland has made great progress of late, has been the reclamation of bogs and waste. Within the last thirty years there has been a gradual but steady conversion of bog and mountain into arable or improved pasture-land. Some of the smaller bogs, where the writer had capital snipe-shooting in 1839, have now disappeared altogether, and many of the larger ones have been encroached upon on all sides, until the acreage reclaimed, though apparently inconsiderable in any one year or any one place, when summed up over the whole country during a period of some length, shows results which are surprising even to those who have watched these improvements in progress. The Census Commissioners, 1841, returned the "uncultivated" land as 6,295,735 acres; and, in 1845, in the Appendix to the Report of the Devon Commission, Sir R. Griffith, General Valuation Commissioner, estimated the acreage of waste lands to be 6,290,000 acres, showing that very little reclamation had taken place between 1841 and 1845. But in 1861 the uncultivated land was reduced to 4,357,338 acres;* so that, in those twenty years, there had been 1,938,397 acres of waste reclaimed, nearly the whole of which must have been brought into cultivation in the sixteen years between 1845 and 1861.

Considerable improvement has been made in various districts by the consolidation of the smaller holdings and the consequent abolition of unnecessary fences. No inconsiderable amount of land has in this way been rendered productive. The old style of Irish fence was a bank formed of earth thrown out of a ditch on each side, the bank being surmounted by quickwood or furze, or more often by nothing at all. These fences necessarily occupied a considerable breadth of land, and were always more or less in a

---

* Census 1861, Part V. p. viii.

crumbling state, so that a moderately active cow could generally change her pasture *ad libitum*; and sheep and pigs could notoriously go where they pleased. The old Irish gate, too, deserves a brief description. Even in those comparatively rare cases where it commences life as a serviceable five-barred gate, it is too often without any other fastening than the ordinary *Irish padlock*, viz., a good-sized boulder-stone rolled against it; and when the gate begins to drag on the ground—as gates have an unfortunate tendency to do, as they advance in years, and when bar after bar gives way from the efforts made to compel it still to open and shut as before—full scope is given for the ingenuity of the Irish character, and it is impossible to help admiring the wonderful variety of expedients resorted to as the gate's constituent elements successively disappear. A bit of bog-pine props the head when the top-bar goes, a small thorn-bush fills the gap when the others follow; and even when all remnants of the original construction have finally departed, Pat's resources are by no means exhausted, and, when the growing crops remind him that it is dangerous to leave them longer defenceless, he builds up in the gateways wonderful piles of loose stones, called "*gauze-walls*," only one stone thick, and consequently full of interstices. The horses and cattle know them well, and carefully avoid touching them, being well aware that if they did, the whole fabric would be down upon them in punishment of their presumption. Providing and maintaining gates for very small fields involves an outlay disproportionate to the value of the produce, but of late years many farms and fields have been enlarged, and a number of very serviceable iron gates have been put up, the advantages of which would perhaps not be sufficiently appreciated, if they were not seen, as they now are, side by side with the old Irish gate just described.

The removal of the unsightly and nearly useless fences above mentioned is a costly process, and can only be gradually effected; but many thousands of miles of them have been levelled in the last thirty years, and the saving of land thus produced is scarcely credible to those who have not seen their size and erratic course. The writer measured one in the Golden Vale, in Tipperary, on grass-land of first-rate quality, and found that a width of twenty-one feet was occupied by the hedge and accompanying ditches. The extent of saving that may in some cases be effected, is well shown by the result of remodelling the Example Farm at Glasnevin, near Dublin, which is vouched for by the able and energetic principal, Mr. Baldwin :—

Land occupied by old fences	13 statute acres.
Ditto „ new hedges	2 „
Saving of land on farm of 180 stat. acres	11 „

Since 1839 a striking change has been effected in the Irish cattle, sheep, and pigs. Yorkshire and Lancashire farmers have long noticed the improvement which has quietly but steadily been taking place in the breeding and quality of the Irish stock brought to their markets, and the equally steady rise in the prices demanded and readily obtained for them. But in order to realise the full extent of the change, it is necessary to traverse some of the best grazing districts in the central and southern counties of Ireland, and see how difficult it is now to find the old long-horned, flat-sided, thick-skinned cow, or the light, active, bony sheep, very good at stone walls, but totally deficient in the placidity of temperament and squareness of form essential to the successful prosecution of a mutton-making career.

Then as to the pigs, a volume might be written, describing first, the good old Irish pig, a huge-framed, flap-eared animal, altogether of the elephantine type, which devoured everything within reach, babies included, and steadily refused for the first two years of its existence to snore and grow fat as a well-conditioned pig ought to do ; and secondly, the modern, roundabout bacon-producer, which has departed so widely from the traditions of its ancestors, that even the ingenious author of a ' Plea for the Celt' could scarcely find a word to say for the modern representative of the " Celtic pig."

Taking the three classes of stock together, the increase in the quantity of meat produced by these better-bred animals, from an equal amount of food, is very great indeed ; and, whilst rejoicing at the result, it must not be forgotten that these great additions to the wealth of a nation do not come of themselves, but require large outlay judiciously made and patiently persevered in, and that those who have taken the trouble and run the risk are entitled to a nation's thanks and praise. It would be difficult to mention the names of any of the most successful breeders of stock in Ireland, without giving annoyance to others, whose names were omitted; but several gentlemen and large farmers might be mentioned, who have spared no expense in obtaining the best blood from first-class English herds, giving as much as 100*l.* for one year's hire of a bull. In this way animals of pure blood have been bred in various counties, which would do credit to the most advanced agriculture; and if as great improvement in the quality of the flocks and herds should be made in the next quarter of a century as has been effected in the last, Ireland would take a very prominent position as a stock-breeding country and be resorted to by improving breeders from all parts of the world.

It is submitted that the proofs now presented of agricultural improvement in the thirty years under consideration are complete and satisfactory, consisting as they do of figures taken from public documents showing that great progress has been made in substituting an improved for an unproductive course of husbandry; that the live-stock has greatly increased in number, and risen in value, and that the "waste lands" have been reduced by nearly two millions of acres. Other minor indications of improvement have also been pointed out, the whole forming a record of progress totally inconsistent with the statements frequently made in public, that the agriculture of Ireland is in a *stationary*, or, as some few assert, in a *declining* condition.

Truth, however, requires it to be stated, that though, viewing Irish agriculture as a whole, improvement is the rule, it is, like other rules, not without exceptions. These exceptions are principally to be found where the holdings are small and the land of the worst description. It is either high up in the hills, where the climate is so ungenial as to make all operations of husbandry precarious, or so near the rock that neither plough nor harrow can work, or a mere encroachment on a neighbouring bog, or a sandy common considered worthless by its owners, and delivered over to squatters for a mere nominal consideration. Under such circumstances as these, there may in most of the counties of Ireland be found specimens of the ancient type of farming in all its primitive simplicity. But to see it in perfection it is necessary to visit the far west, where, among the wild hills of Galway, Donegal or Kerry, a traveller may, by avoiding the beaten track, withdraw from all traces of modern civilization, and, by a slight exercise of imagination, fancy that he has gone back several centuries in the world's history, and that the huts and habits of the people, like the grand old mountains around them, have remained unchanged from the time of Con of the hundred battles or Niall and his train of hostage kings.

Authors of a somewhat romantic turn, returning from a summer excursion in these regions, have frequently endeavoured to enlist the sympathies of the stay-at-homes in favour of the existing state of things, and to persuade the public that the welfare of the nation in general, and the Celtic race in particular, was altogether dependent· on their retaining the facilities they possessed for lounging through life in the enjoyment of sunshine and tobacco, rendered all the more agreeable by the periodical necessity for exertion at seed - time and harvest. If one of the duties of Government were to provide objects for the gratification of the æsthetic tendencies of this highly refined age, a good deal might be said in favour of maintaining a few colonies of this kind for the gratification of poets, painters, and other worshippers of the picturesque, for certainly nothing can be more charming in its way than many a valley among these western hills. But in order to ensure a "grand succès," all the accessories must be carefully selected. The time, for instance, must be August or early September, when the heather and dwarf furze are in full bloom. There must be no village near enough to mar the effect by its sights and sounds, but a straggling white-washed cabin or two in the half distance, and a few half-clad boys and girls near enough to exhibit the wild beauty of the Connaught youth, and above all on some slightly rising ground a group of peasant women, with their erect carriage and far-famed crimson petticoats, not to mention their classical abhorrence of any superfluity of apparel. Surely with these stage properties, and an unlimited allowance of sunshine, any experienced manager ought to be able, either by word painting or on canvas, to get up a " furore " on behalf of such arcadian scenes, and to organize a crusade against improving landlords, consolidating agents, and all other mammon-loving barbarians who might seek to spoil the picture. Grand stage effects, however, are only imposing at a distance ; a few feet nearer and the illusion is gone ; go behind the scenes and all is tinsel and varnish ; and alas for the poetry of Irish peasant life, a near approach destroys that too. Even sunshine will not remove the traces of too close an intimacy with the cow and the pig ; and when the stern realities of winter drive the inhabitants of an Irish cabin to close and continuous shelter, the entire want of cleanliness and studied absence of ventilation produce their inevitable consequences—disease and misery.

These peasant occupiers of small holdings form the sole exceptions to the rule of progress which is applicable to all other classes. As they were thirty—might it not be said three hundred—years ago, so are they now ; shrewd, impulsive, warm-hearted, dirty in their persons and habits, not because they like dirt, but because they hate trouble ; capable of extraordinary exertion on a great occasion, but speedily relapsing into a dreamy lounging life, relieved by occasional violent excitements of love and hate. Every true lover of his country longs to see their numerous good points

brought out and made more useful both to themselves
and to the nation. *But how to do it?* Who will
undertake to solve this most difficult of problems?

It is plain that no improvement in their habits can
take place without a previous improvement in their
circumstances; and how are the circumstances of men
cultivating three or four acres of bad land to be improved? If work could be found for them the difficulty would disappear, but in the districts where the
majority of these small occupiers reside there is no
one to hire them. The largest farms are very
small, and their occupiers employ little labour out of
their own families. They also know well that men
who have grown up to consider themselves farmers,
on however small a scale, who have always been
masters of their own time, and who would necessarily
have to attend to their own crops at seed-time and
harvest, when their labour was most valuable, would
not be labourers who could be profitably employed by
farmers working hard for their own living. In the
immediate neighbourhood of large landowners' residences, a certain number are employed, and a few
more might be, but this would meet a very small
portion of the difficulty.

Government works of drainage and reclamation on
a large scale have been suggested, but these works to
be effective would require trained and able-bodied
labourers, unless undertaken for benevolent purposes
alone, which could never be relied on as a national
resource, general experience having shown that

charity work has so demoralizing an effect on the labourer that it ought never to be employed, except possibly in the case of some great national calamity. Failing employment for their spare time, could any improvement in cultivation be introduced which might increase the produce of the land, and thus leave a larger balance available for the occupiers. The writer has devoted his most anxious attention to this point, but without success, and he is thoroughly convinced that the only possible cure is the gradual consolidation of these small holdings. Spade cultivation is a valuable auxiliary, and no agricultural labourer's cottage should be without a sufficient quantity of land to enable him to provide vegetables for his household, and, if possible, maintain a pig; but *on bad land no man can maintain himself and his family in comfort by spade cultivation alone.* By trusting implicitly to the potato crop, he may raise *food* enough in an average season, but in a bad potato year he must be brought to the brink of starvation; and even in good years there can be no sufficient surplus to provide clothing and the other requirements of civilized life, even where the rent is merely nominal. There are, no doubt, thousands in Ireland who are striving for existence on these terms; and the result is that they inhabit huts which are worse than the wigwams of savages, and that their life is one of continual struggle and privation. Even if sufficient produce could be raised without horse labour to keep the occupier and his family in tolerable comfort, the women must necessarily be degraded into beasts of burden, and convey on their backs (as is too frequently seen in the wilder districts) the crops, the indispensable turf, and the lime and other tillage required to maintain the fertility of the land.

Hence it is obvious that where men have no other resource but the land they occupy, the first step towards raising them in the scale of civilization must be to increase the size of their holdings by consolidation, until they are large enough to maintain a horse. Looking at the question in an agricultural point of view, the minimum sized arable farm ought to be placed much higher, as there are great advantages in having sufficient land to keep a pair of horses steadily at work, and to effect this, three ought to be the quorum, that the plough may not be stopped whenever produce has to be marketed, turnips carted, or any of the irregular work of the farm performed. But in Ireland there are numerous dairy farms on which there is little arable land, and if a farmer have one horse he can generally borrow another from a neighbour similarly situated, whenever his small modicum of ploughing, harrowing, &c., must be attended to.

It thus appears that to the smallest class of occupiers fixity of tenure would be a curse instead of a blessing, and any legislation tending in this direction would be only throwing additional obstacles in the way of measures really calculated to improve their condition. *What is really wanted is to raise the status of the most improving men by increasing the size of* their holdings, and to ensure liberal compensation to those who, from time to time, give up their land.

This raises another difficult question, viz :—How to estimate the compensation to be given to men for improvements effected in the land by their own labour? In many cases a cottier is allowed to occupy land at a nominal rent, on the condition of reclaiming a certain acreage in a limited time. This is an arrangement frequently made by a tenant-farmer with his labourers, and some of these bargains are very hard ones; but the landlord has not the same excuse for driving hard bargains which the tenant frequently has, and wherever an owner wishes to dispossess a small occupier, who has spent much time and labour in clearing and reclaiming his land, even where it has been very imperfectly done, and will, much of it, have to be done again, a very liberal valuation should be made of the improvement effected.

In framing any legislative enactment which shall secure to an outgoing tenant compensation for his improvements, the case of these small holders will be the most difficult one to meet. Perhaps the best mode of arriving at a just appreciation of the claims of the respective parties will be by tracing the operation step by step. It must be remembered that all good land has been long ago brought into cultivation, with the exception of a small portion of that still covered by bog, which need not be taken into account at present. The reclamation of waste land now is generally effected either by adjoining tenants who do the work at those seasons when ordinary farm work is not pressing, or by labourers, who in like manner devote themselves to it whenever they cannot obtain regular employment. There is a third class of improvers who used to be the most numerous of the three, but who are now rapidly decreasing, viz., those known by the name of "squatters," who were for one reason or another allowed to settle on the land, sometimes paying a slight acknowledgment, sometimes nothing at all. These squatters' first care was to erect a mud-hovel, without a window or chimney, and covered with sods resting on a few rough pieces of bog-pine, a residence in every respect inferior to a fox-earth or rabbit-burrow, these last always having a rise at the end, which ensures the occupants a dry bed, a luxury by no means always to be found in a squatter's cabin.

On one occasion, two friends of the writer taking shelter in one of these cabins, when benighted, had great difficulty in extracting their horse from the one apartment in which it shared with them the owner's hospitality, in consequence of its being *bogged in the middle of the floor*.

Having built his house and buried a few bushels of seed potatoes, the squatter had nothing to live upon until potato harvest, and accordingly he closed his house and set off on a tour in England, to raise a little money by haymaking, harvesting, or hop-picking, whilst his wife and children wandered about Ireland picking up a precarious existence, by asking the "*loan*" of a few potatoes from the more thriving farmers. If an accurate and circumstantial account of the wanderings of some of these poor souls could be published, probably it would surprise every one, even the "Faculty" themselves, to learn how much privation and starvation the human frame could endure and still return to tell the tale.

Under favourable circumstances the steadiest and most industrious of the squatters gradually reclaimed a sufficient portion of land to create a diminutive farm; but the potato disease made a squatter's life impossible, and there are comparatively few of them now left.

Three classes of improvers have been described, but their claims to remuneration on leaving their holdings may be treated alike, as they are all founded on the expenditure of time and labour. The reclamation of the kind of land here called waste would not pay as an agricultural operation. If it had to be performed by day work, the cost would amount to far more than the value of the land when reclaimed, and it cannot be done by contract, as no contractor would undertake it at such a sum as it would answer to the owner to pay. The only way in which it can be done without loss is bit by bit as an occupation for a man's spare time. For instance, a piece of land is covered so thick with stones that the soil is *scarcely visible*. Travellers by rail between Ballinasloe and Galway well know that this is not an exaggerated expression. A reclaimer begins by throwing and wheeling the stones into heaps, and gradually brings to light sufficient land to grow grass for a cow; but the sheep grazing on the adjoining mountain make free with his incipient pasture, and he has to enclose his little field, probably only a few perches in extent, with a wall made out of the surplus heaps of stones. If things go well with him, he probably enlarges his boundaries at a fresh expenditure of labour. He has also to build his own house, and provide shelter for the cow and the pig. It is not wonderful that under these circumstances the live-stock who play so important a part in reclaiming the waste should be temporarily admitted to share the warmth of the cabin, and what once becomes a habit is never altered. It certainly is desirable in the interest of the nation that the improvement should not stop at the stage where the improver is arrested by arriving at his neighbour's boundaries; but when two of these small occupiers meet, and one is selected to carry on the doubled farm upon which it will answer to have better buildings, and thus train up the rising generation in improved habits, the one who either moves to another part of the United Kingdom and becomes a labourer, or emigrates and becomes a landowner in another country, ought to receive a sum of money which will enable him to make a fair start elsewhere.

The landowner's view of the matter is somewhat of the following kind:—"The land has been let for years at a nominal consideration, and is now worth some shillings an acre. The occupant has laid out nothing but his labour, and has been paid for that by occupying the land much below its value. As to the buildings, they will be all pulled down when the land is annexed to the neighbouring farm, and the fence walls, crooked and ill built as they are, will put the next tenant to great expense in their removal. It would be hard, therefore, that I should have to pay for so-called improvements which I would rather be without." The public interest, however, must eventually overrule all other considerations, and though it is clearly a great national object that the civilization of the people and improvement of the land should go on, it is equally important that the rights of property of all kinds should be protected, not the rich man's property alone, but also the poor man's only wealth—his labour. To turn out an industrious improving cottager without compensation, would be in many cases to throw his maintenance on the rates, and would on all accounts be diametrically opposed to the public interest, and although his fence walls and his buildings may be incumbrances on the land *now that it is improved*, they were the machinery by which its improvement was effected, and the man who constructed that machinery ought to be paid for it.

The case above described is one where the improvement chiefly consists in the removal of superfluous stones; the same argument, however, applies *mutatis mutandis* to the levelling and drainage of wet boggy land, and still more forcibly to those cases where, from the shallowness or barrenness of the staple of the soil, the reclamation is effected by bringing on to the land bog-earth or other material sufficient to make it grow a crop. The difficulty, however, of estimating the proper value of improvements gradually effected through a course of years still remains, and it is submitted that where landlord and tenant cannot agree as to the proper amount of compensation on the termination of a tenancy, it would be a reasonable mode of getting rid of these complications to allow the tenant to claim a limited number of years' rent. This is intended to apply to small occupations alone, say those of which the rent does not reach 10*l*. The larger farms will require to be dealt with differently.

It has frequently been suggested that much may be done by education to improve the rising generation of small occupiers. No doubt much is being done in this direction both in the National Schools and in the denominational schools of the different religious persuasions; but as soon as the young people are sufficiently instructed to be able to compare their positions with that of the labouring classes elsewhere, they are no longer willing to wear rags and live in pigsties, and the majority of them emigrate. Is this necessary ? There are parts of the country where labour is becoming scarce, and where a comfortable maintenance might be obtained by a working man, but where is he to live ? There is in Ireland a great scarcity of the snug cottages so generally to be found in England wherever labour is required. Many landlords are already building them, and it is to be hoped that many more will follow their example, but it is notorious that the landlords, as a rule, have been either unable or unwilling to provide them. Their tenants have naturally followed their example. The common custom has been to encourage the labourers by some slight assistance to build their own houses, and the badly constructed mud-cabins so prevalent throughout the country are the result.

It would be worse than useless for the classes immediately concerned to indulge in mutual recriminations for what is past. There is much work now to be done, requiring all shoulders to the wheel, if the young active labourers are to be kept in the country. An Englishman may be pardoned for giving a strong opinion in favour of the labourers' houses being provided by the landlords; but where they are not, and the tenants are willing to build cottages of an improved description, the fullest security should be given them by law that, on any change of tenancy, the then existing value should be repaid them.

The point arrived at then is, that education and better dwellings may do much to improve the habits of the rising generation, but that the existing occupiers of very small holdings can only be raised in the social scale by gradual consolidation of their small patches of land; and, further, that those who give up their land at their own, or their landlord's desire, should receive liberal compensation.

Pauperism and the Poor Law.—No reference has yet been made to the increase or decrease of pauperism during the period under review. The Poor-law was established in Ireland in 1838, but some years elapsed before the workhouses were completed and the machinery could be considered in working order. In 1846 and the subsequent years of famine, a severe strain was put upon the new system; and, even in 1850, the aggregate number who received relief during the year were 805,702 in-doors, and 368,565 out. From this time there was a continuous decrease until, in 1859, the number of paupers reached its minimum; the aggregate number receiving relief in that year having been reduced to 153,706 in-doors, and 5425 out. Three disastrous agricultural seasons followed, and raised the numbers by successive annual steps, until 1863, when the aggregate numbers were 288,713 in-doors, and 28,911 out. No useful purpose would be answered by comparing the present number of paupers with those relieved during the famine years, or during the preceding period, when the Poor-law was gradually taking its place as a national institution; but any fluctuations which have occurred within the last few years deserve careful scrutiny, to ascertain to what extent they may be considered indications of corresponding vicissitudes in the condition of the labouring classes. Some disappointment has naturally been felt that the number of paupers has not been reduced to a lower point since 1863, although the general prosperity of the country has been rapidly advancing. The last Annual Report of the Poor-law Commissioners (dated 31st March, 1869), contains tables giving the average daily number of persons receiving relief *in* and *out* of the workhouses for the last seven years. The figures composing the following Table are extracts from the larger tabular forms given in that Report :—

	Average Daily Number receiving Relief in Workhouses.	Average Daily Number receiving Out-door Relief.
1862-63	55,610	6,263
1863-64	58,203	7,859
1864-65	55,808	8,748
1865-66	52,121	10,040
1866-67	50,241	12,205
1867-68	53,017	14,940
1868-69	53,757	16,862

On the strength of these figures it has been argued that the condition of the labouring classes has really not improved of late, notwithstanding the rise in wages and increase of employment, which have been undeniably taking place simultaneously with the above increase of pauperism. There has been a steady advance, it will be observed, in the amount of out-door relief administered, and on this point the Report of the Commissioners speaks very plainly. It says (p. 13),—

" Under such circumstances, when the number of workhouse inmates shows a decrease, as in the present season, indicating a decided improvement in the general condition of the lower classes, the sustained increase in the numbers receiving out-door relief must not be permitted to interfere with that conclusion, *as it really indicates nothing more than a change of views on the part of Guardians of the Poor in favour of the extension of out-door relief.*"*

In another part of the same page, the Commissioners say,—

" Not more than half, however, of the 163 Unions can be said to have yet adopted it as a regular branch of their system of relief. . . . ."

After so decided an expression of opinion on the part of those who have all the facts before them, and are so well qualified to judge of their true bearing, it is unnecessary to offer any additional proof that the steady increase in the amount of out-door relief administered during the last ten years, is totally independent of any alteration in the condition of the labouring classes.

During the last two years the inmates of the workhouses have somewhat increased, when a diminution might have been expected; but the increase is not large, and cannot be considered of any great importance, when it is remembered that there is in Ireland not only a labouring class, but a class below the labourers—viz., the small occupiers, whose case has already been investigated at length, and whose condition is inferior in every respect to that of the workman receiving wages. These small holders so

---

* The italics are the author's.

long as they continue to exist in any large numbers, must always swell the number of inmates in the workhouses, whenever an unpropitious season diminishes the productiveness of their crops; and, on such occasions, the number of applicants for relief can only be kept within moderate bounds by the great repugnance felt to entering the Union-houses, and becoming regular paupers. The same objection is not felt to the receipt of out-door relief, and, if unfortunately the Boards of Guardians throughout Ireland should follow the example set by one-half of their number, there seems no reason to doubt that nearly the whole of this class will in every bad potato-year be on the Union-books. As civilisation advances, there is an increasing tendency to abolish those holdings which are too small to maintain their occupiers with any certainty except in favourable seasons; and nothing more prejudicial to the social advancement of the country can well be imagined, than an attempt to prop up and perpetuate an otherwise untenable position, by applying to that purpose the hard earnings of the small farmers who pay so large a portion of the rates. The real labourers are undoubtedly in a far better position than they were in twenty years ago, and though there must always be some among them who are overtaken by unavoidable misfortune, or become victims to their own excesses, it may safely be asserted that the pauperism of Ireland would be reduced within much narrower limits, were it not for the existence of the class who occupy small patches of land quite inadequate, on the average of years, to support life.

Rents and Farmers' Profits.—The preceding estimate of the increase in the general prosperity and resources of Ireland during the last thirty years would be incomplete if it did not include an estimate of the farmer's present position as to rent and profits. It has frequently been stated, that, in consequence of extreme competition, rents in Ireland have been forced up to an unnaturally high rate, when compared with the rents of similar land in England, or with the intrinsic value of the land itself. As this question has an important bearing on the present inquiry, great pains have been taken to examine it in all its bearings, by a very extended examination of the crops at various stages of maturity, of the condition of the cattle grazing on the pastures, of the nature of the soil and climate, and of the cost of conveying the produce to market. Every opportunity has also been embraced of obtaining the opinion of practical land valuers, conversant with the letting value of land on both sides of the Channel. The result arrived at has been, that on a general average of the provinces of Leinster, Munster, and Connaught, the rents in Ireland are lower than those in England, by the full difference between the English and Irish acre, viz., that they are as 5 to 8. The position of the province of Ulster is so different from that of the three others, as to require separate consideration.

It will readily be understood that, even assuming the foregoing estimate to be a good approximation to the average rent of extensive districts, it may be very wide of the mark when applied to individual farms, or even estates.

The best land in Ireland is in general let low. There is grass land in Tipperary, Meath, and some of the other grazing counties, for which the writer would only be too happy to give 60$s.$ the *statute* acre, if they could be added to his home-farm in Yorkshire, and could bring the Irish climate with them. Much of this land is let at 40$s.$ to 50$s.$ the *Irish* acre, though fattening two sets of cattle during the year, or producing what would be considered in England fabulous crops of hay. As a natural consequence, the graziers are, at the present high prices of fat stock, making much money. The price of butter and of young store stock is also very remunerating, and the rent of dairy farms being generally moderate, the small dairy farmers are, as a rule, doing well. In their case, however, there is a certain amount of drawback, from having, in most cases, to provide their own buildings. If the English standard of farm buildings were adopted, this would be a great burden, but the Irish estimate of the necessary cowhouses, stables, &c., is by no means extravagant.

The "grazing" and "dairy" farms include a large portion of the whole country. In 1869 the grazing land amounted to 10,046,877 statute acres, whilst the arable land (including fallow, and meadow, and clover) was only 5,596,824 acres, or not much more than half. When allowance is made for the fact that almost all the dairy farms, and many of the grazing farms, include some arable land, it is evident that only a small portion of the country consists of what would ordinarily be called arable farms. Though, however, the strictly arable farms are few, those containing arable land are many, and the returns from this portion of the land show on the average much less profit than from the grass and other green crops.

The price of corn, now that the markets of the world are accessible to every commercial nation, never rules high for any length of time, and the climate of Ireland makes the harvesting of grain, in many seasons, expensive and precarious. The great rise in wages of late years has also fallen heavily on the arable farmer, so that, on the whole, it may be said that the dairy farmers are making money, and the grazing farmers getting rich, but the arable farmers probably not doing much more than making both ends meet.

If English farmers had their rents reduced in the proportion of 8 to 5, they would rapidly grow rich. What special circumstances are there in Ireland to prevent the great body of Irish tenants doing the same? It is generally believed that it is the want of security of tenure which prevents the occupiers of land from laying out their capital sufficiently freely to develop the capabilities of the soil. This is, no doubt, one cause, and a very influential one, where farmers are unfortunate enough to hold under needy, grasping owners; but these form a small minority of the landlords of Ireland; and other causes must be sought for, of more general application. One of these is to be found in the habits of the farmers themselves. They are ready and quickwitted, and therefore good men at market. They are also first-rate stockmasters, and feed the cow and the pig far better than they do themselves; but they are not good plough-farmers. The cardinal points of good arable farming are *deep cultivation, frequent stirring of the soil, early preparation of the land intended for crop,* so as to command a seed time in precarious seasons, and *war to the knife against weeds.* In all these points the Irish arable farmer is too often deficient. Neither his ploughmen nor his teams are equal to a deep furrow on strong land, and being underhanded they are, of course, behind time, and may frequently be seen preparing the land when they should be sowing it. As to the weeds!!! The general result is, that the arable land throughout the country produces much less than it would do if the horses had beans, the men bacon, and the farmer himself a little more foresight, the benefit of which would be reaped in the first crop without requiring any appreciable addition to the capital embarked in the farm.

The gross receipts being thus reduced by defective or dilatory farming, a further deduction has to be made from the farmer's profits in order to provide interest on the original cost of the farmhouse and offices, which in Ireland are generally constructed at the tenant's expense. This has been made the ground of serious reflections on the landlords, as if they neglected their duty in not providing the buildings requisite for the proper occupation and management of their farms. But, when fairly considered, it will be seen to be an almost necessary consequence of the very small holdings which, previous to 1846, were so general throughout Ireland, and which are still numerous enough materially to affect this question. On an estate visited this summer, there were above 1000 tenants, and the average rent paid by each did not quite reach 10*l.* If the landlord were to build a moderate-sized house and offices on each of these holdings at an average cost of 200*l.*, and charge 5 per cent. on the outlay, it would *double the rent*, an arrangement which the tenants neither could nor would accept. If, on the other hand, the English or Scotch view were to be taken, that the landlord ought to provide all buildings without any special charge on that account, the *rent would be annihilated.*

Mr. Fitzgibbon, one of the Irish Masters in Chancery, has published some valuable statistics of the estates managed by the Court of Chancery, which show that the case above mentioned is by no means so exceptional as might at first sight appear. Mr. Fitzgibbon says:—

" The estates of lunatics and idiots, the estates of infants, and estates involved in litigation, are taken into the management of the Court of Chancery. Of these estates there are at present (1868) 655 in the custody of that Court..... On the 452 estates in my office, there are 18,287 tenants paying rents amounting to 330,809*l*. On the 203 estates in the other offices, there are 10,294 tenants paying rents amounting to 162,248*l*. This shows an average rent payable by each tenant of about 17*l*. a year." *

In a subsequent part of the same work it is stated that—

"Upon an estate producing a rental of 13,193*l*., there are 2493 tenants, being an average for each tenant of about 5*l*. 6*s*. a year." †

The owner of a rental of 13,193*l*. would no doubt be considered a wealthy man, but building houses for 2493 tenants would absorb the fee-simple value of the estate. It is evidently, therefore, a case for compromise. The tenants can do the work much more cheaply than the landlord, and they are content with much less accommodation for both themselves and their stock when they make their own buildings than when the landlord provides them. On the other hand, a tenant cannot be expected to lay out his capital without remuneration, and this liability is no doubt one of the principal reasons for the rents in Ireland being so much lower than in England.

Any one travelling in Ireland in 1869 must have

---

* 'Ireland in 1868.' By Gerald Fitzgibbon, Esq., p. 130.
† Ibid., p. 131.

been struck with the attitude of expectation which pervaded all classes connected with land. Landlords, who would at any other time have willingly granted leases to their tenants, were afraid of compromising themselves by entering into any permanent arrangement, until they knew what the provisions of the Ministerial Land Bill would be. Tenants, on the other hand, who were anxious for leases, had been led by hustings and platform speeches to hope that the Government measure would give them better terms than any lease they were likely to obtain from their landlords. All agricultural enterprise was, therefore, paralysed, and men of the most opposite opinions concurred in thinking it extremely desirable that the next session of Parliament should not pass without placing the land laws of Ireland on a settled basis.

Land Tenure.

After conversing unreservedly with numerous tenant farmers in different parts of the country, the writer is of opinion that the majority of this class are sensible, practical men, who do not desire extreme measures, and that their opinions are not fairly represented by the leaders of the Tenant-Right agitation. As, however, the moderate men have not put forward any programme of their own, it is necessary to examine carefully the demands made in their name at the numerous meetings held to discuss the subject.

Fixity of Tenure is the most prominent of these requirements. At a meeting of the Cork Farmers' Club, held in August last, at which representatives from several similar clubs in the district were present, and when the writer was kindly allowed to submit certain questions for the decision of the meeting, it was unanimously decided that nothing less than fixity of tenure would meet the views of those present. Fixity of tenure was defined by the speakers on that occasion to mean, that so long as a tenant paid his rent, and committed no wilful waste, the law ought to confirm him in the undisturbed possession of his land; also that the rent he was to pay should be fixed, not by his landlord, but by the State, subject to revision at stated intervals, and further, that whenever the period of revision arrived, no improvement made by the tenant should be taken into account, but any alteration in the rent should be based on the altered prices of produce, or other extraneous circumstances unconnected with the tenant's exertions or outlay of capital. This definition will probably be generally accepted as a fair statement of the views of those who advocate "*Fixity of Tenure.*"

Fixity of tenure, then, means that the landlord shall be permanently deprived of the power of selecting the tenants who are to occupy his land, and of fixing the rent at which he is willing to let it. The power of planting and cutting down trees must also be transferred from the landlord to the tenant, for when the agricultural produce of the land is permanently secured to the occupier, it would be clearly unjust to allow the landlord to plant trees which would diminish that produce, or to cut down trees which had been planted by the tenant, and were valued by him for ornament or shelter, or had been nourished by the land to the exclusion of other crops which belonged to him. The landlord would thus lose all control over the letting, cultivation, and management of the land, and all connexion with it except in the character of mortgagee. He would retain the title deeds as security for the payment of his rent-charge, as a mortgagee does for the repayment of his loan, but he could take no interest in the prosperity of an estate the entire control of which had been taken out of his hands, and he would no longer have any inducement to lay out money in permanent improvements, with the rare exception of opening out and working minerals where they existed. The management of mines is, however, so entirely unconnected with the occupation and cultivation of the surface-soil that it may be safely omitted from the present inquiry. All other kinds of improvement, such as building, draining, planting for shelter, reclamation of waste, would cease to be performed by the landowner when once permanent possession of the land had been given to the occupier; for it is scarcely probable that the landlord would ask permission from his tenant to lay out money in improving his holding, on the speculation that at the next periodical revision the Government valuer would in consequence give him a remunerative addition to his rent-charge; nor could it be done without asking permission, as it would evidently be unjust to a tenant in perpetuity to allow improvements to be made against his will, which were to be made the foundation for a claim to a permanent increase of rent.

As a general rule, landowners are not too anxious to lay out money in improvements, even with the certainty of a reversionary interest in them. Were that reversion transferred to the tenant by Fixity of Tenure, it may be safely assumed that landlords' improvements would be discontinued, that the expenses of estate management would be cut down to a minimum, and that absenteeism would greatly increase.

The tenants' position would undoubtedly be improved by Fixity of Tenure; but to justify depriving landowners of all their rights of property excepting a mere rent-charge, and making a present of these rights to the tenants in possession, would require a strong case of State necessity, or a clear prospect of such great and general public advantage as to outweigh all ordinary considerations. The advocates of Fixity of Tenure maintain that its adoption would ensure a great increase in the produce of the soil. If this were proved, and if it could also be shown that with a rapidly-increasing population the food produced in a country of great agricultural capabilities like Ireland was decreasing, or had even remained stationary, through a considerable period of time, that would indeed be a position justifying strong measures. But it is submitted that not one of these propositions is capable of proof. *The population is decreasing : The agricultural produce is increasing;* and the question whether or no that rate of increase would be accelerated by Fixity of Tenure is open to the gravest doubt.

With reference to the first of these assertions, the decrease of the population is, of course, undisputed. The increase of the agricultural produce (stock and crop) when tested, not by the results of a single season, but through a period of some length, is equally indisputable, and has been already proved by extracts from the official returns. The third proposition is the only one which admits of argument, and there are in Ireland great facilities for bringing it to the test of experience. Holdings in perpetuity at fixed rents are common in most parts of the country, and on many estates there are farms which have been leased for ever at rents which, though possibly fair when the leases were granted, are now much below the letting value of the land. There may be seen side by side, under precisely similar circumstances of soil, climate, markets, &c., the tenant-at-will paying a full rent and the perpetuity-tenant a very low rent; and if Fixity of Tenure possessed the power attributed to it of stimulating its possessor to extraordinary exertion by the certainty of reaping the fruits of his industry, nothing surely would be easier than to make converts to the doctrine by inviting them to look on

" this picture and on that." On one side of the fence is the perpetuity holding, where it may be anticipated that the advantages of Fixity of Tenure will be conspicuously visible. Buildings in good repair, land in good condition, the whole farm drained, levelled, squared, a picture of comfort and good husbandry. Over the wall may be seen the poor tenant-at-will living from hand to mouth, almost afraid of sowing lest he should not be allowed to reap, longing to make improvements on his land, but too uncertain of his tenure to venture upon the outlay, and not even daring to put his land into condition lest his rent should be raised.

Alas for those who put their trust in hustings and platform speeches! The foregoing contrast between the tenant-at-will and the holder in perpetuity, illustrated by every conceivable variety of argument, and aggravated by the utmost exaggeration of expression, has been going the round of Ireland for the last twelve months, yet no one thinks it worth his while to ask, *Is it true?* It would seem at first sight simply impossible that the statements so confidently made, and so incessantly repeated, of the total difference between the conduct and condition of the tenant-at-will and the holder of a perpetual lease, should be untrue, when it was so easy to ascertain the fact. In no part of Ireland would it be necessary for an inquirer to travel many miles in order to compare on the spot the style of farming and actual position of the two classes. The writer has, not in one, but in many cases, where

he had been told that the two kinds of tenure might
be seen in juxta-position, made it a special request
that he might not be informed which was which, in
order that the crops and general appearance of the
farms might tell their own story. But he found it
impossible to distinguish between the two kinds of
tenure by their outward appearance, and his guesses
were just as often wrong as right. The fact is, *there
is no perceptible difference between them*. There are good
farmers and bad farmers, both amongst the tenants-
at-will and the tenants-in-perpetuity, and it would be
easy to find select cases which would favour each side
of the question; but taking the country fairly through,
it may be safely asserted that the tenants-at-will and
the tenants-in-perpetuity farm equally well or equally
badly according to the district in which they happen
to reside.

But though this is true of the perpetuity-holder,
who pays a moderate (though low) rent, an exception
must be made of those cases where the tenant holds
his farm for ever for a mere nominal payment, and
which he rightly considers as substantially his own
land. These farms are notoriously in a worse position than any others. Portions of them have been
alienated in various ways. Squatters have been lo-
cated on some of the wettest and poorest bits of land,
on condition of giving so many days' work by way of
rent. Other parts of these farms have probably been
leased, bequeathed, or even sold; and a very common arrangement is to mortgage a field, the mort-

gagee cropping it until the loan is repaid. This repayment is often deferred so long that the mortgagee declines to give up possession, or he crops the field without manuring it, until the land will produce no more, when he throws it up, and requires another field or his money. As these arrangements are frequently verbal, the complication of interests becomes perfectly inextricable, and leads to endless disputes.

The advocates of Fixity of Tenure argue that all such alienation might be prevented by special enactment. It would, no doubt, be easy to insert clauses in an Act of Parliament, making all such arrangements legally invalid. *But they are legally invalid now;* yet they are continually occurring. It could scarcely be intended that sub-letting should be made penal, and, even if it were, it would be impossible to carry such an Act into operation, as no one would give evidence. If one man is determined to sub-let part of his farm, for a certain consideration, knowing that the law will not sanction it, and another can be found to give that consideration, though well aware that the law will not assist him in obtaining possession of the land, or recovering his money if cheated; or if another, on condition of receiving a certain advance, agree to let his neighbour crop his best field until he can repay him—what power on earth can prevent them? Even now, with tenancy-at-will, it requires all the vigilance of the most active resident agent to keep such transactions within moderate limits. Fixity of

Tenure would put an end to the landlord's interest in the matter, and who would take his place? The good of the State undoubtedly requires the prevention of unlimited subdivision of holdings, and the consequent certainty of periodical famines. But who is to represent the State? Are the police to intrude into a man's private affairs, and forbid him to receive money from his neighbour for the temporary possession of a field? How are the police to become cognizant of the matter? They may see A ploughing in B's field; but B being a consenting party, is it conceivable that any State officials should have authority to interfere? If so, the introduction of such an amount of Paternal-Governmentism would be infinitely worse than the present state of things.

If holders in perpetuity were greatly multiplied by Act of Parliament, they would, in all human probability, act very much as holders in perpetuity do now, which makes it specially important to look closely into their present position. There are perpetuity-holders who pay no rent at all, and, by lapse of time, have become owners in fee. Some good instances of this kind may be seen in the County of Kerry, near Tralee, where, on the commons of Ardfert, squatters have had possession without payment sufficiently long to become proprietors. Here "la petite culture" has been carried on for many years under the most favourable circumstances. No rent to pay,—the soil easy to cultivate, and requiring no drainage. What, then, is the present position of these commons?

There is one townland (in England it would be termed "hamlet" or "township") called the "West Commons of Ardfert," to which the writer paid a special visit, and which merits a particular description. In the Official General Valuation of Ireland its area is given as 61 acres, 4 perches; and its rateable annual value (1869) 32*l.* 15*s.* for the land, and 24*l.* for the buildings; total, 56*l.* 15*s.* Of the 61 acres 4 perches of land, 7 acres, 2 roods, 23 perches are held by three non-resident proprietors, leaving 53 acres, 1 rood, 21 perches to be shared amongst 39 resident owners. *The result, then, of peasant ownership of this hamlet through a considerable period of years is that each proprietor on the average owns 1 acre, 1 rood, 19 perches of land, and the state of cultivation arrived at is such as to be valued at 10s. 9d. per acre!* The crops, the houses, and the people, were in no way distinguishable from those ordinarily met with on similar patches of land held by tenants-at-will.

On one occasion, two adjoining farms in a northern county were visited, one of which, held in perpetuity at a fixed rent of 2*s.* 6*d.* per acre, was in a slovenly, neglected state; the other showing signs of enterprise and improvement, though held at will at a fair rent. The writer accosted the occupier of the latter farm, congratulating him on the general appearance of his land. The farmer commenced with the customary grumble about rent, rates, &c., but, when his fine herd of ten dairy cows was praised, he went off at score like a true son of the soil. "One of his cows was the greatest wonder in all Ireland." "This field he had drained at his own cost." "Those fences he had levelled," &c., &c. In short, he was a favourable specimen of a thriving, industrious, improving tenant. The writer remarked that, notwithstanding his being overpowered with rent and taxes, he could at any rate beat his neighbour at farming; when he made this significant reply: "'Deed, your Honour, he's no farmer at all, it's his own land; *he can live 'asy whilst I must work hard.*" Looking at the two farms, it was not difficult to decide whether it was most for the national interest to multiply the "*Live 'asys*" or the "*Work hards.*"

The evidence adduced up to this point all tends to shew that the existing holders in perpetuity do not, on the whole, raise more produce from their land than tenants-at-will. What reason, then, is there to expect that if by Act of Parliament the tenants-at-will were suddenly converted into perpetuity men, they would rapidly change their style of farming, and greatly increase the produce of their farms? How would they set about it? The weakest point in Irish farming is the want of attention to details, which increases in intensity as the farms decrease in size. Even on the smallest holdings the occupiers make great exertions to collect manure, and work hard on their land until the potatoes are in; but after that, they too often subside into a state of comparative inactivity, as if they had done their part, and nature must do the rest. They will look on calmly and see the weeds gradually smothering their crops without stirring hand or foot to prevent it. Possibly they may have a lurking respect for these genuine children of the soil, whilst they feel themselves, whether Celts or Saxons, to be but invaders. At all events, the fact is indisputable that the small holder, whose whole wealth is in his little fields, will look on with apparent indifference day by day, and week after week, while weeds of every kind run a neck-and-neck race with their corn and potatoes, all striving to get their heads the highest, and to secure the largest share of the fertilizing substances which are so limited in quantity, and which it has cost the farmer so much labour to procure. If any remark is made by a stranger, the answer is ready—"*Sure there's not such land in Ireland for growing weeds;*" but the thought never seems to occur to his mind that some of his long-legged boys and girls who are idling by the roadside would with their active fingers weed the whole potato-field in a very few days, and that it would be more to the purpose to do it himself than to fold his arms whilst the mischief is in progress, and then grumble all winter at the potatoes taking up so "light and scanty." On many thousand acres there was a loss this season of more than the whole rent from this cause alone.

The same remissness is observable in haymaking operations. For want of employing sufficient hands, many of the fields are not mown till there is a great loss of quality in the grass, and even when made into hay, and put into large cocks, it is left in that state for weeks, until, when ultimately removed, it grieves the heart of a true farmer to see the dry mildew flying off like a cloud, and to know that a large portion of what was once fine provender is reduced to such a state that its presence materially injures the rest. On being remonstrated with, the farmer's invariable answer is, " There are no men to be had ;" which, being translated into plain English, means, " We do not choose to pay the requisite wages." Why do sixty or seventy thousand souls leave Ireland every year at the present reduced rate of emigration ? Simply because they cannot get sufficiently good wages to induce them to stay at home. If a railway were to be made in any county in Ireland, the contractor would soon get together as many hands as he wanted. He employs no strange or occult arts, yet he succeeds in bringing men together by hundreds, where the farmers say they cannot collect a few score. The fact is, that bad haymaking is simply a case of bad calculation. The farmer wants to get in his hay without hiring additional men, or without raising his rate of wages. The wish is natural enough ; he could not live by farming if he did not economise his expenses in every practicable way. But if by cutting his grass too late, and leaving his hay exposed too long, he sacrifices more of the value of his crop than he saves in wages, he is, of course, a loser by the transaction ; and that this is the case is but too plain.

Both hay and after-grass are materially injured, but the loss on the former is frequently from 20 to 30 per cent. of its value. Unluckily for the hay, or, rather, for the animals who live upon it, the damage done is unseen when the haystack is at last completed, and it is difficult to trace the consequences of its diminished nutritive qualities to the dairy or the butcher's shop. *If farmers, and especially farmers' wives, drank hay-tea, the evil would soon be remedied.*

Fixity of tenure, however, would afford no special facilities for good haymaking or for clean husbandry, and tenants-at-will would rather seem to have the greater inducements to make the most of the growing crops, which they can, at all events, call their own, however precarious may be their tenure. But it is stated that fixity of tenure would induce farmers to lay out capital in the land, which, without security of possession, they are afraid of doing. Before arguing this point, it should be stated that the tenancy-at-will here mentioned is not tenancy-at-will as at present existing, which is universally condemned; but tenancy-at-will modified by such changes in the law as shall secure to the tenant full compensation for his outlay. Bearing this in mind, it may be asked in what way a farmer would probably proceed who wished to invest more capital in his land. The most obvious methods would be by *raising the condition of his land* or by *permanent improvements*. The first method would lead him to purchase more tillage, and to grow more restorative

F

and fewer exhaustive crops. But this is a course which is equally open to the tenant-at-will and to the tenant-in-perpetuity, and is, in fact, the line that would be taken by every farmer who properly consulted his own interest, as good farming will always pay better than bad, whatever may be the nature of a man's tenure.

There is then only the outlay of capital on permanent improvements to be considered. Building, draining, fencing, reclamation of waste, come under this head, and tenants-at-will cannot be expected to lay out their money in this way unless certain of liberal remuneration. These permanent works are more especially landlords' improvements, and the landlords have in past times done comparatively little in this way; but there has been a great increase of late in both the ability and the disposition of landowners to carry out improvements at their own cost, or to help their tenants in making them, giving them, at the same time, liberal agreements to indemnify them for their share of the expense. Fixity of tenure would take away all inducement for the landlords to continue this course; and the case stands thus:—Would tenants having fixity of tenure, if unaided by their landlords, make more permanent improvements than would be effected by tenants-at-will if secured by legislative enactment, full compensation for their outlay, and assisted by such landlords as were able and willing to give a helping hand? Looking at the conduct of the existing perpetuity-holders, the writer is disposed to back the "*Work hards*" against the "*Live 'asys*," either with or without the help of the landlord's purse.

If the foregoing reasoning be sound, Fixity of Tenure would not cause any increase in the produce of the land, and the argument breaks down which has been chiefly relied upon to support this great invasion of the rights of property. It is also deserving of special notice that the position in which Fixity of Tenure would place the great body of tenants would be that of nominal landowners without the power of making large measures of improvement now possessed by landlords in virtue of their rentals. It has always been supposed that the owners of estates so deeply encumbered that the rents were absorbed by the interest of mortgages and other settlements were great impediments to the improvement of the country, yet Fixity of Tenure would place all the present tenants-at-will in a precisely similar position as permanent holders of the land subject to the payment of a full rent. The one great result, therefore, of Fixity of Tenure, which seems absolutely certain is, *That it would sever all useful connexion between the present landowners and their estates, and create a numerous body of small, deeply encumbered landholders in their stead.*

Compulsory Leases.—Another form of Fixity of Tenure has found favour with some writers under the name of *Compulsory Leases*, and the advocates of those leases have suggested that the compulsion to grant them might cease after the lapse of a certain number of years, by which time they suppose that the state of the country would be so much improved that they would be no longer required. If, however, the State should compel landowners to grant leases avowedly to induce the tenants to invest capital in their farms, and should subsequently refuse to compel the renewal of the leases when the tenants had completed their buildings and other improvements, this would indeed be an alteration in the law which left things worse than it found them. If, on the other hand, the State should require the renewal of the leases, it is scarcely necessary to add that *compulsory leases, compulsorily renewed,* are neither more nor less than "Fixity of Tenure," though called by another name.

Tenancy-at-Will.—The greater part of England and Ireland is held by tenants-at-will. It is difficult to find any other argument in favour of this mode of letting land. English landlords are accustomed to it, and see it work smoothly and satisfactorily, so that probably very few of them have ever considered what a one-sided arrangement it is. Of all kinds of business, agriculture is the one which requires the most patience and perseverance, and which brings in the slowest return. Even in England a man who enters on a farm generally finds the land out of condition, and on the ordinary four-course system must spend his money freely for four years before he can get round his farm and restore it to a productive state. The expenditure, which it takes him four years to make, will, when the process is reversed, take him at least four years to recover. This is on the supposition that the in-coming tenant has sufficient capital to be able always to make the necessary outlay at the right moment. Most tenants, however, find it more convenient to go on quietly improving through a series of years, instead of doing it all in the first rotation, which, of course, strengthens the argument in favour of a lengthened tenure. But the *shortest* period in which a man able and willing to farm well *can* put his land into condition is four years. A large outlay is also required on entering a farm, in providing what may be called the working plant, horses, implements, &c., and on this a great loss would be incurred if the farmer were obliged to sell it again without several years' use. If, then, a tenant must spend much for some years before he can begin to reap the fruits of his outlay, and if his expenditure cannot be recovered in less than a four years' rotation of crops at the very least, how, in the name of fairness and common sense, can he be asked to take the land subject to a six months' notice to quit without any compensation for the capital which he must leave embarked in the land? Yet this is the actual position of the great majority of tenant farmers in England at the present moment. Landlords maintain that the power of dismissal is never put in force in the case of a deserving tenant, but that it is necessary to retain the means of protecting themselves against a bad farmer who is injuring the land. So that, to secure absolute safety to the landowner's property, the tenant is called upon to embark *his* capital in the land without the slightest protection or security! Truly the case will not bear arguing, except on the ground that the landlords have on the whole made such a moderate use of this unreasonable power that no grievance of any magnitude has arisen in consequence. It is found, by experience, that tenants-at-will hold their farms longer and at lower rents than those who have leases, which English farmers are not slow to discover. When all parties are content, it is true wisdom to "leave well alone."

In Ireland the position is entirely different. There the tenant-at-will is *not* satisfied with his position, and claims through his representatives that his case shall be heard and decided by the British Parliament. Not only does he urge this now, but so long ago as

"in the years 1835 and 1836, and again in 1843, Bills were presented to the House of Commons, of which the object was to secure for tenants compensation for any outlay which they make of a permanent nature upon their farms." *

It seems almost incredible that a quarter of a century should have been allowed to elapse without any redress for so undoubted a grievance, after such able and impartial men as those composing the Devon Commission had reported that,—

---

* 'Report of Devon Commission, 1845,' p. 17.

"Although it is certainly desirable that the fair remuneration to which a tenant is entitled for his outlay of capital, or of labour, in permanent improvements, should be secured to him by voluntary agreement rather than by compulsion of law; yet, upon a review of all the evidence furnished to us upon the subject, we believe that some legislative measure will be found necessary in order to give efficacy to such agreements, as well as to provide for those cases which cannot be settled by private arrangement. *We earnestly hope that the Legislature will be disposed to entertain a Bill of this nature, and to pass it into a law with as little delay as is consistent with a full discussion of its principle and details.*" *

In considering the nature of the grievance complained of, it will be found, Cerberus-like, to have three distinct heads, the *first* of which regards the ordinary cultivation and management of land. The *second* relates to improvements, such as draining, clearing land of stones, reclaiming bog, &c., which, though forming no part of ordinary farm work, are yet undertaken by the occupier with a view to profit. The *third* includes all improvements, such as buildings, fence walls, roads, &c., which do not make any return to the tenant, but are undertaken by him as being absolutely essential to the proper occupation of the farm.

The *first* mode in which tenancy-at-will creates a grievance has been already explained to be inherent in the very nature of a tenure which makes an occupier liable to lose his farm at six months' notice,

---

* 'Report of Devon Commission, 1845,' p. 17. The italics are the author's.

although he cannot recover the outlay he has made on his land in less than a complete rotation of crops. This part of the grievance might be remedied by Mr. Caird's suggestion,—

"That a tenant holding without written lease should be secured in possession by presumption of law (except for failure to pay rent) for an equitable term, say five years, sufficient to recoup the expenditure necessary to a proper system of cultivation." *

This remedy is, however, open to the very serious objection, that during the whole period that the notice is running, it would be the tenant's interest to reduce the condition of the farm to the lowest possible point, and to commit spoil and waste, unless vigilantly watched, which would lead to unpleasant feeling on both sides, ending in disputes and law proceedings, perhaps even in violence. It therefore seems desirable to provide an alternative course; and whilst considering this point it will be assumed as a just and sound basis for legislation that no tenant ought to be displaced from his holding without such a length of notice as will enable him to recover the capital embarked in the land in the ordinary course of cultivation, and further, that such length of notice may fairly be measured by one ordinary rotation of crops, so that in Ireland the length of notice would be five years. In order to provide an alternative plan which would

---

* 'The Irish Land Question,' by James Caird, p. 23.

obviate the loss and inconvenience inseparable from so lengthened a notice to quit, it will be necessary, in the first place, to calculate what sum would fairly represent a tenant's annual profit. Probably no closer estimate could be made of so variable a quantity than that it is on the average about equal to his rent, and therefore that a gross sum equal to five years' rent would be an equivalent for a five years' notice. A legal enactment drawn up to carry out this view would provide that no tenant holding without lease should be dispossessed without *five years' notice*, or the *customary six months' notice and the payment of a sum equal to five years' rent*.

The most obvious objection to this proposal is that the compensation could be claimed equally by the good tenant to whom it is only a fair reimbursement of previous expenditure, and the bad tenant who has lowered instead of raising the condition of his farm. This objection, when closely examined, however, is less serious than it appears at first sight; for, in the first place, it would constantly diminish as cultivation improved, and, after reading in the preceding pages the record of results realized by Irish farmers during the last thirty years, they must be faint-hearted indeed who have no faith in the future of Ireland's agriculture. *Secondly*, the objection would be no disparagement to the plan in the eyes of Irish tenant-farmers, but would probably be considered by them as a merit rather than otherwise, as being in unison with their present ideas and practice.

The occupiers will be the most difficult class to satisfy by a new law, as, in addition to the natural dislike which all farmers have to change, Irish tenant-farmers have, by one means or another, placed themselves in a better position than the law gives them, and they will certainly not abandon this position unless fully satisfied that they shall obtain something better. On the other hand, this method has some strong recommendations; one of which is that, though based upon what is equitably due to any man who farms fairly, it will in Ireland be generally considered an equivalent for "good will," thus causing it to be acceptable to the tenant. It will also, by adopting an unvarying number of years' purchase, obviate the danger which threatens the landlord's property so long as an arbitrary payment continues to be demanded which has no recognized measure or limit.

One of the chief difficulties of framing a measure which shall apply to all occupiers of land in Ireland, consists in the wide difference existing between the means and position of different members of this numerous body; and the writer would suggest that they should be divided into three classes, according to the amount of rent paid. Any division of this kind must, of course, be an arbitrary one, and the merits of the scheme proposed must not be considered to rest in any degree on the exact figures named, which can be easily altered if thought desirable. By making a definite proposal, however, the object with which the classification is suggested will be more clearly brought out. Subject to such modification, it is proposed that the *first class* should consist of occupiers paying less than 10*l.* rent; the *second* of those paying 10*l.*, but less than 50*l.*; and the *third* of all paying 50*l.* and upwards. The case of the first and most numerous class has already been dealt with, and it has been suggested, on public grounds, that no occupier of a holding of this value should be dismissed without a payment equal to five years' rent. The alternative, therefore, of five years' notice or five years' rent would not apply to this class. The second class includes the great body of the working farmers of the country, as, though in actual numbers they are not equal to the preceding class, there are included in the first class a great number of labourers having mere potatoe gardens, and residents in towns occupying small plots of land who cannot in any reasonable sense be considered farmers. It is, therefore, most important that the measure proposed should be one which will be favourably received by the shrewd, practical men who form the great bulk of this division, and it is suggested that to this class be given the option of demanding five years' rent or five years' notice. The third class is comparatively a small one. Out of the total number of occupiers of land in Ireland, amounting to 608,864, there are only 35,955 who pay a rent of 50*l.* and upwards, and as they are for the most part men of capital and independent position, well able to take care of themselves, it is proposed that in this class the option of giving five years' notice or five years' rent should be transferred to the landlord.

Such an arrangement as this would, it is believed, work fairly for both landlords and tenants. In the case of all holdings of the first and second class, the landlord might be called upon to pay five years' rent when the tenant gave up possession, but he would have no difficulty in finding a new tenant who would willingly pay this sum for peaceable possession. No charge would therefore be thrown upon the landowner. But in the case of large farms, it would in many cases be difficult, in some impossible, to find tenants who would give five years' rent on entry, and the landlord ought therefore to have the option of giving the longer notice instead of paying a large sum of money. The evils of a long notice have already been pointed out; but if the law required the long notice or the large payment, it would be a strong inducement to landlords to give leases for reasonably long terms (say twenty-one years), which would probably be accepted by the bulk of the occupiers of this class.

The *second* reason for considering tenancy-at-will a grievance, is that in Ireland tenants who drain, reclaim bog or waste, or otherwise improve their holdings, most commonly do so at their own cost. Those improvements only are here referred to which the occupier undertakes with a view to profit. As a general rule, it would be unwise in an occupier to undertake improvements which would not pay him more than bank interest for his money; and, fortunately, there are few investments which pay better than drainage, and other agricultural improvements, if judiciously and effectively carried out; drainage is sometimes known to repay the whole outlay in a single crop, and it may safely be assumed that all claims on the part of tenants to reimbursement of their outlay on this class of improvements may be fairly met by a sufficient number of years' occupation without increase of rent. A great deal of evidence was taken by the Devon Commission on this point. There was, as might be expected, considerable difference of opinion amongst the witnesses, of which the following may perhaps be considered a fair sample:—*Mr. John Donnelan Balfe*, farmer (County Meath), says,—

"I think 21 years would be sufficient to compensate a tenant for any improvement on land, provided it was of a medium quality."*

James Johnston, Esq., landed proprietor (County Donegal), was asked with reference to the operations of trenching and thorough draining at a cost of 7*l*. per acre,—

"Do you consider that 7 years will repay a man for such an agricultural improvement?"—"I am perfectly certain of it."†

Mr. Joseph Lambert, farmer (County Mayo),—

"I would say that a 14 years' tenure would operate as a sufficient encouragement to a tenant to improve, and that

---

* 'Digest Devon Commission,' p. 182.   † Ibid. p. 100.

a man having that term unexpired should not have any claim for remuneration."*

Major T. Scott, landed proprietor (Londonderry), stated that on a field of 20 acres one improved crop after draining nearly paid the whole expense of thorough draining, and that a lease of seven years would repay any improving farmer.†

Mr. John Wilkin, farmer (County Tyrone), says,—

"Upon some ground which would need draining exceedingly, I should say that three or four crops would almost repay a man; upon other ground, which did not need it so much, it might require the length of a good lease for a man to be repaid one-half."‡

In Scotland, where agriculture is conducted in a more strictly commercial spirit than probably in any other part of the world, and where the profit and loss of each operation are carefully calculated, 19 years' leases are extremely common, and tenants do not hesitate to undertake draining and other improvements at the commencement of a term of this length, without the slightest prospect of any reimbursement of their outlay beyond what they can obtain from the land during the continuance of their occupation. The writer has had some experience in draining and other agricultural improvements, and is of opinion that 21 years' occupation without increase of rent would be a liberal return to the tenant for any improvement of the kind now under considera-

---

* 'Digest Devon Commission,' p. 192. † Ibid. p. 102.
‡ Ibid. p. 105.

tion. If a strictly agricultural improvement would not reimburse the tenant with a handsome profit in 21 years, it ought not to be undertaken.

The *third* grievance inflicted by tenancy-at-will refers to improvements of an unremunerative character. In Ireland the tenant is generally expected to provide the house and farm buildings chiefly or entirely at his own cost. It has been already pointed out that, in consequence of the smallness of the holdings, this arrangement is almost a matter of necessity. But if the landlord declines to erect the buildings because it will not pay, and the tenant has to undertake this necessary but unremunerative work, it follows, as a matter of ordinary justice, that he should either have his land at a lower rate for such a term as will make the reduction of rent an equivalent for the outlay, or that he should, on leaving his farm, be repaid the existing value of the buildings, boundary walls, &c., erected by him.

The practical operation of these suggestions will perhaps be most clearly perceived by applying them to a few cases representing different classes of farms.

No. 1 may be assumed to be a fine grazing farm in Meath or Roscommon, which the landlord wishes to take into his own hands. Rent 500*l.* per annum. In this case the tenant has been put to no expense in buildings or other permanent improvements, and, on receiving notice to give up his farm, he has five years' further enjoyment of his holding, during which he may, at his leisure, make arrangements for the future. On the other hand, the landlord, knowing that he cannot materially injure the land, and that it would be difficult to find a tenant who would advance the large sum required for immediate possession, would prefer letting him hold on for five years to making him a large money-payment on his own account. On a farm of this kind a tenant-at-will would spend nothing on his pastures, and even grass land, unless of first-rate quality, the extent of which is very limited, would deteriorate under a long course of such treatment; but if certain of five years' tenure after receiving notice to quit, the occupier would be sure of being reimbursed for any outlay on top-dressings, or in the destruction of docks, thistles, and other weeds, so that the stock reared and fattened on the ten millions of acres of permanent pasture in Ireland would, in all probability, be greatly increased, to the manifest advantage of the public.

No. 2. A moderate-sized arable farm. Rent 30*l.* In this case the tenant has put the land into fair condition, for which he will be entitled to receive five years' rent = 150*l.* He has also built a house and offices; present value 100*l.* He could therefore, on the receipt of a notice to quit, claim 250*l.*, if he resolved to give up his farm at the end of six months, and in the present state of opinion in Ireland on this subject, he would probably decide to do so. If farming improved, and the land were brought into higher condition, a tenant would probably conclude that he could make more than 150*l.* by retaining possession to the end of the five years' notice, in which case he could only claim the value of the buildings. By the time, however, that he had made so decided an advance in his system of cultivation, he would feel the importance of having a lease; and, in the altered state of the law, his landlord would probably be equally glad to give a lease for a moderately long term to an improving tenant of this kind.

No. 3 is a farm of similar size and description to the last, and let at the same rent; but, the tenant is a bad farmer, and has his land poor and entirely unimproved. The landlord wishes to put it into better hands, and gives him notice to quit. He has, however, built his house, an inferior one; present value 30*l.* In this case the tenant would certainly decide to give immediate possession and claim the five years' rent = 150*l.*, in addition to the 30*l.* for his buildings. Notwithstanding the bad state of the land, however, a tenant would readily be found to give the 180*l.* for what he would consider "goodwill." Should the farm belong to an improving landlord, he will probably endeavour to secure an improving tenant, by a promise of some outlay in the way of building, draining, or other needful works.

No. 4 is a small holding in an average state of cultivation (rent 20*l.*), chiefly grass, which is used for dairy purposes; but the farm includes a considerable plot of rough mountain pasture, of which the tenant has drained, limed, and reclaimed 10 acres, at a cost of 10*l*. 10*s*. per acre, calculating his own time spent on the work at the current rate of daily wages. Supposed additional letting value of improved land 10*s*. 6*d*. per acre. This is on the supposition that the additional produce from the reclaimed land is worth 1*l*. 1*s*. per acre, of which 10*s*. 6*d*. represents additional rent to the landlord and 10*s*. 6*d*. tenant's profit. The improvement of the land has, on the average, been effected ten years before the receipt of the notice. It is assumed that twenty-one years' occupation, without increase of rent, would be a fair indemnity for the cost of improvements of this character; so that, neglecting interest, each year's occupation would, in this case, diminish the tenant's claim by 10*s*. per acre. He would therefore, if he left at the end of six months, be entitled to five years' rent = 100*l*., added to such a proportion of the cost of reclamation as would represent the unexpired portion of twenty-one years. In this case ten years have expired, and, consequently, eleven years remain to be paid for at 10*s*. per acre per annum, and the account would stand as follows:—

Tenant's claim on leaving at the end of six months.

	£
Five years' rent	100
11 years at 10*s*. per acre per annum on 10 acres of reclaimed land	55
Total	155

If he elected to remain in possession five years after

receipt of notice to quit, the claim of five years' rent would disappear, and the bill for reclamation would be reduced by five years' more occupation to 30*l*.

No. 5 is a small holding under 10*l*. This, it has been already shown, ought, on account of the poverty of the occupier, to be dealt with on public grounds, and no option given to the landowner; but, in all cases, a minimum amount of compensation equal to five years' rent paid on eviction, increased by the present value of any buildings erected by him.

Leases.—A considerable variety of leases may still be found in Ireland. Leases in perpetuity, leases for long term of years, leases for lives, and leases for lives and concurrent terms of years. There are also many modern leases for 21, and some for 31 years. The leases for long terms (99 years and three lives, for instance) are almost universally relics of byegone times, when the power of leasing was grossly abused. Even within the recollection of men now living, the condition of the bulk of the tenant-class was such that the collection of rent was a difficult and uncertain process, and quite foreign to the natural habits of the rollicking, devil-may-care squireen of famous memory; and he was too ready to turn over to the tender mercies of a middleman a numerous tenantry and extensive acreage for a very moderate amount of certain rent. The middleman was generally a close shaver, whose intimate acquaintance with the position and habits of his victims enabled him to turn to account both the necessities of the

landlord and the fears of the tenant. He tempted the
owner in his hour of need by an irresistible offer of
ready cash, and secured for himself, at a nominal
rent, a lease in perpetuity of many a broad acre, or
varied his amusement by distraining on the tenants,
and if they were so poor as to be quite intractable,
he farmed them off in small lots to sub-middlemen,
whose own habits of life were such as to give them a
perfect knowledge of every weak point in the position of the wretched cultivators of the soil, and of the
exact amount of produce that could be squeezed out
of them without actually stopping their breath. The
extent to which this was carried is almost incredible
at the present day. A fine farm was pointed out, in
the County of Kerry, held now by one tenant under
the head landlord, which in the last generation was
leased and sub-leased to lessees, sub-lessees, sub-sub-
lessees, &c., until *five descending grades of tenants'
tenants were interposed between the landowner and the
actual cultivators of the soil!!* The rent paid to the
landlord was 100*l.* per annum. The amount extorted
from the occupiers 500*l.* per annum!!

If leases for equally long terms were granted now,
the same process would recommence at once. The
temptation is too strong to be resisted. Farmer A
has two sons and two daughters. It is far easier to
bequeath the farm to the two sons by a stroke of the
pen, than to lay by money for the younger, and,
what is of still more importance in his eyes, it enables
him to add 50 per cent. to the fortune of each of

his daughters. It is difficult for an Englishman to appreciate the full force of this motive in the breast of an Irish farmer. The amount of the daughters' fortunes is a matter of the keenest pride and rivalry among neighbours. Let it once be known that A will give 200*l.* to each of his daughters on their marriage, and he is placed in the class of "warm" well-to-do farmers, and takes a position among the bachelors of the district which is much coveted, and which too often leads a man to rob the land of its due in order to swell the balance at the bank. Even the son's wife's marriage-portion is frequently added to his sisters' fortunes, instead of providing comforts for the newly-married couple's *ménage*.

Another kind of temptation would be equally irresistible. The rapid rise of labourers' wages during the last twenty years has pressed hardly upon the smaller farmers. By giving up to a labourer land enough for a house and potato-field, he plants at his own door a working man whom he is not obliged to employ all the year round, and from whom he receives by agreement a certain number of days' work instead of rent. The farmer thus avoids paying money-wages, and forgets that he adds one to the number of struggling families who can get no employment for six months in the year, and must go upon the rates whenever their potato crops are deficient.

It may be thought that a stringent covenant in

the lease would prevent this subletting and subdivision of land; but if the lease be a long one the day of reckoning is far off, and the landlord, having little prospect of the farm coming into his hands during his own life, too often leaves his successor to take care of himself. Nothing but a forfeiture of the lease would be effectual; and even this must not be subject to the verdict of a jury, for the majority of country juries consist of farmers, and the forfeiture would never be enforced by them. Taking into account the character and habits of the great body of occupiers of land, the writer is strongly of opinion that long leases would *not* be beneficial to Ireland; but, on the contrary, that they would hold out much less inducement to improve than would be afforded by leases for twenty-one years, or even by tenancy-at-will, guarded as previously explained. The advocates of long leases argue that twenty-one years is too short a term to reimburse a tenant for building. This is readily admitted, and, in the suggestions for compensation already given, it is proposed that all buildings and other unremunerative works should be valued at the termination of a tenancy, and the amount of the valuation paid to the tenant, whatever may have been the duration of his enjoyment of them. This would be a direct inducement to the tenant to make the buildings substantial, and to keep them in good repair. If the question of length of lease were thus kept clear from the difficult subject of building, other improvements would be fully met by a twenty-one years' lease; and a term of this length would keep up a landlord's interest and disposition to assist in works of an expensive nature, whereas long terms would close the owner's purse by destroying the prospect of his ever deriving any benefit from the improvement of the land so leased. There are many tenants who, in the present state of feeling in Ireland, would not accept leases for twenty-one years; on the other hand, there are many who would, and the number of these would in all probability greatly increase as the conviction spread that the land question was settled for many a long year, and that nothing was to be gained by agitation, however violent.

Ulster Tenant-Right.

Ulster Tenant-Right or *Goodwill* is one of those strange anomalies which, if not known to exist, would be deemed simply incredible. A buyer of land in Ulster has to pay as many years' purchase for it as in any of the other provinces; and there, as elsewhere, before the transaction can be legally completed, a sum of money must be paid to the National Exchequer, in return for which an official stamp is affixed to the deed of transfer, which extends to the purchaser the protection of the State in case of the infringement of any of his legal rights of ownership. The law declares that any proprietor may obtain possession of his land at the end of the term fixed by any lease or other legal instrument held by the tenant, and, in the absence of any such legal demise, then at the end of six months' notice duly given. But, when the new proprietor proceeds to take possession according to law, he finds his claim directly resisted by another possessor of the land, who, though only called the tenant, has paid, in many cases, as much for peaceable possession as the nominal owner has for the fee simple; and he intimates, pretty plainly, that peaceable possession, if again required, can only be had on the same terms as before.

Here, then, is *one* of the results of Ulster Tenant-Right.—That two claimants for possession of the land are brought face to face; one relying on legal right, the other openly defying the law and placing his trust in secret combination and threatened violence. Before proceeding to extremities, however, the antagonists closely scan their respective powers and chances of success, and—low be it spoken—the uniform result is a conviction that the law is unable to protect those who rely on its support. The new proprietor, therefore, not being able to pay a second time the value of the estate, or willing to accept the death's head and cross-bones alternative offered him by a "*Friend and Well-wisher*," sulkily submits to the inevitable, and abandons the idea of occupying the land himself. By and by he discovers that the property is let much below its value, and he congratulates himself on the prospect of obtaining some salve for his wounded feelings by an increase of rent.

He is not the first, however, to discover that the land is worth 40*s.* per acre, though let at 20*s.*, and the 20*l.* per acre paid by the tenant on entry was based on this foundation. When, therefore, he gives notice that the rent will in future be raised from 20*s.* to 30*s.* per acre, the same attitude of antagonism is assumed as before, with the same result, except that a small *concession* is made by the tenant and the rent is increased by 2*s.* 6*d.* instead of 10*s.* per acre.

The *second* result, then, of tenant-right is that the owner of land worth 40*s.* per acre generally lets it at 20*s.*, rather than run the gauntlet of the Vigilance Committee on whose decision it will depend whether an increase of rent, however small, is to be allowed or resisted. No doubt, many proprietors assert that the low rate at which their land is let arises solely from their own good will and pleasure, and is in no way whatever influenced by the probable decision of any secret Committee, whose existence even, in their particular district, they question, if not altogether deny. The most implicit trust must be placed in the *bona fides* of these statements, but that they are mistaken may be easily shewn. The writer does not hesitate to affirm that land in Ulster is generally let at little more than half its agricultural value; and, although individual proprietors may have a fancy for receiving only 50 or 60 per cent. of what would be a fair rent for their land, it cannot be supposed that the bulk of the landowners of this large province hold these peculiar views, especially when it is borne in mind that the amount of rent which they lose is not gained by the tenant, but represents the interest, or more commonly a portion only of the interest, of a sum extorted from him on entering the farm.

If any proprietor is sufficiently confident in his own opinion to venture to test it by actual trial, let him announce an increase of 50 per cent. in his rents. Very few weeks will pass before he will have satisfied himself not only of the existence of a Vigilance Committee which watches over his district, but of how little power he really has of fixing the rent to be paid on the land which yet he believes to be entirely under his own control.

The most strange part of this strange story, however, still remains to be told; which is, that a considerable proportion of landowners and land-agents in Ulster uphold tenant-right, and describe it as a system which *obtains more rent for the landlord, which improves the cultivation of the land, which gives security to the tenant, and peace and tranquillity to the district.*

The first point, then, to be examined is—Does Ulster Tenant-Right obtain more rent for the landlord? This naturally resolves itself into the two considerations: whether the land is rented higher in Ulster than elsewhere, and whether the rents, on the whole, are better paid? As to the first, there can scarcely be any doubt that, having regard to the *quality* and *condition* of the land, rents are lower in

Ulster than in the rest of Ireland; in other words, the landlord's rent represents a smaller portion of the produce of the land than in the other provinces.

With reference to the question of punctuality of payment, tenant-right is undoubtedly an additional security for the recovery of arrears of rent in bad times. In good times like the present, rents are well paid everywhere. Many agents were kind enough to show the writer the office-books, in which were recorded the actual receipts and arrears in different townlands, or even on whole estates, and the arrears were frequently represented by one figure out of a rental of some thousands of pounds. Taking the rate at which the land is let and the arrears both into account, there is little doubt that the amount received from an estate in Ulster is less than from one of equal productiveness in any of the other three provinces.

The second question relates to the cultivation of the land. That the cultivation is better in Ulster than in any other district in Ireland of equal extent is at once admitted. The farming is better, and, as a natural consequence, the condition of the land is higher. It may, in fact, be assumed that the gross produce of the soil is greater in Ulster than in the other provinces with as much certainty as that tenant-right exists in Ulster; but to what extent is the one fact influenced by the other? The writer believes that there is very little connexion between the two. There are several reasons for Ulster being well farmed ; the most influential of which is the existence of manufactures in the province. It is not necessary to quote English or Continental instances to prove that manufactures of any kind raise the standard of farming and improve the condition of the agricultural population in the adjoining district. In the year 1869 this assertion will probably pass unchallenged ; but in Ulster the manufactures are of a kind to produce a more than ordinary effect. Probably no branch of manufacturing industry affords so much cottage employment as the linen manufacture, from the first preparation of the raw material to the completion of that very popular product, "Irish linen."

On the other hand, the land and climate of Ulster are peculiarly suited to the growth of flax ; and small farmers with large families can cultivate that crop with greater profit than those who have to pay in cash for the labour so largely required at all stages of its growth. There are other smaller industries, too, such as the embroidered-muslin trade and shirt-making, especially for South America, which, in the city of Derry, employs many hundred hands, and sends work into the country to a distance of 30 miles ; thus providing employment of the best kind for the small farmers' wives and daughters at their own homes. The improved cultivation of Ulster may also be partly due to the difference of race, which more or less prevails throughout the Settlement Counties, and is observable, not only in the personal appearance of the people, but in the greater neatness of their dwellings and the more improved state of their farms. The same difference of appearance and cultivation is observable in those parts of the County of Wexford colonised by the Welsh. Possibly it may be attributed to the fact that settling in Ireland was known to be no child's play, and that only the men of stoutest hearts and strongest limbs volunteered for it. On this supposition, the Irish climate—notoriously favourable to human life—must be credited with having maintained unimpaired through eight or ten generations the mental prowess and bodily powers of those select men.

The reasons alleged are sufficient to account for the higher state of cultivation in Ulster, independently of the effect of tenant-right. Nor is it easy to discover any connexion between improved farming and tenant-right. Its most evident effect is, undoubtedly, in the opposite direction. Most of the farms given up are in very bad condition, and require large and immediate outlay; but an incoming tenant parts with his ready money just when he is most in want of it, or, worse still, has to borrow at a high rate of interest. In too many cases, therefore, he is unable to cultivate his farm profitably; and, beginning by starving his land, ends in being starved by it.

Another beneficial result claimed for Tenant-Right is Security of Tenure. This is a still more groundless assertion than the last. If anything in connexion with the Irish land-question is certain it is that it is easier for a landlord to part with a tenant in Ulster than in any other part of Ireland. But in this province the odious name of *Eviction* is avoided, and it is simply termed, as in England or Scotland, a *change of tenant*. As a rule, landlords have no wish, either in Ulster, Munster, Leinster, or Connaught, to turn out a man who farms fairly and pays his rent; but when a tenant is going to the bad, whether oppressed by usurious interest on the heavy sum paid for tenant-right, or from any other cause, it is far easier to remove him in Ulster than in the other provinces. After taking all he can out of the farm, and selling peaceable possession for as much as any one will give for it, he goes quietly, *because he knows that there is nothing more to be got*. Evictions on a large scale do not affect men in the rank of farmers; they apply only to small cottiers and squatters, who may be found in considerable numbers in the county of Donegal, but in most parts of Ulster sweeping evictions of this class are simply impossible, not on account of tenant-right, but because the evictions were made wholesale *two or three centuries ago*. It is therefore asserted broadly that, so far from tenant-right giving security of tenure, *it acts precisely the other way, and makes it easier for the landlord to remove an objectionable tenant*. Nor does it give a tenant security for his capital. Instead of investing his money in good stock, implements and manures, and thus producing heavy crops, which could be valued on the termination of his tenancy, or improving his holding by drainage, or even buildings, for which, by a simple legal enactment, he could be secured adequate compensation, he gives an arbitrary sum, regulated by the intensity of a competition which is always varying, for an ideal right, which, by a change of landlord or agent, may at any moment be materially curtailed. He is, therefore, haunted by the idea that the large sum he has paid without security may never be recovered, and anxiously watches every step taken by either landlord or agent, that he may detect, and take timely measures to thwart, any intention of encroaching on his precarious property. In this, as well as in its other aspects, therefore, tenant-right keeps up between landlord and tenant a spirit of watchfulness and distrust, which produces an unhealthy and unnatural state of society.

The fourth cardinal virtue attributed to Tenant-Right is its tendency to secure peace and tranquillity to the district. Diplomatists have, for some years past, had much to say in condemnation of a state of *armed peace*, which is described as costly, and as raising in the countries immediately concerned uneasy anticipations of future trouble, which are eminently unfavourable to the production of wealth or the cultivation of the useful arts. The present state of Ulster resembles very closely an armed peace. *It is costly to the landlord ; it is costly to the tenant;* and it maintains *an antagonism of interests* between the two which *generates uneasiness and suspicion.*

That it is costly to the landlord, by preventing his receiving more than from 50 to 60 per cent. of the real value of his land, is so plain to the eye of every farmer, that one consideration only will be offered in support of the assertion. It is, however, a conclusive one, viz., That any tenant-farmer who has the opportunity of subletting a portion of his farm never thinks of adding a few shillings only to the rent per acre he pays, but *doubles* or *trebles* it, without being troubled with any misgivings that he is overweighting *his* tenant. Does this sub-landlord, who has occupied the land himself, know what it is worth or does he not? It may be said that, though the land is let below its value, tenant-right is not the cause. But no other cause has been assigned except the one previously mentioned, that some landlords prefer receiving 20*s.* to 40*s.* per acre for their land, and, as this applies to a limited number only of remarkable idiosyncrasies, it may be dismissed without further notice. That the tenant who has land to let has neither scruple in asking nor difficulty in obtaining double the rent received by the head landlord is notorious ; and it may safely be asserted that if tenant-right could be abolished by a stroke of the pen, with its ugly train of Riband Societies and Vigilance Committees, and a sound system of tenant-compensation substituted for it, there would no longer be any obstacle to the land being let at its real value.

Tenant-Right is also costly to the tenant. That it cripples his means, at a time when he has most need of all his available resources, is undoubted; and as this is one of the worst features of tenant-right, it is worth probing thoroughly. Tenant-right or goodwill is, of course, only paid when a tenant leaves his farm. Why does he leave it? In *almost all* cases because he cannot pay his way. The writer was unable in all the four provinces to obtain half-a-dozen well-authenticated instances of *solvent* tenants having given up their farms. Let a case be supposed in which a tenant is about to leave who gave 500*l.* for goodwill when he entered on his farm, and that he receives the same amount on leaving, of which he devotes 300*l.* to paying his debts, and with the remaining 200*l.* goes to America. It is claimed as one of the great recommendations of tenant-right that it thus constitutes a sort of reserved fund, out of which the tenant pays his debts, and has a balance left to pay his outfit as an emigrant. But if he had kept his 500*l.* in his own possession, instead of paying it away for goodwill, he would have been able to discharge all his liabilities as they arose, so that he *would never have been in debt,* and *need not have emigrated.* Again, it is argued that what the landlord loses in rent the tenant gains; but this is not true, as the tenant-right rises in proportion to the lowness of the rent, and it thus becomes impossible for a tenant to obtain a cheap farm wherever Ulster Tenant-Right has its full swing. Rent and interest on the sum paid for goodwill, together make an *extreme* rent in many cases—a *full* rent in all. Some reasoners shut their eyes to the numerous cases in which incoming tenants are ruined by borrowing at high rates of interest the large sums they have to pay for goodwill, and pin their faith altogether on those instances where the incoming tenant has money enough of his own to pay for the goodwill without borrowing. But even on this supposition, the tenant is a great loser; as, if he had invested his 500*l.* in the farm, it might reasonably have been expected to make a gross return of 10 per cent., which would, in the majority of cases, have made the whole difference between farming at a profit or a loss. Ulster Tenant-Right is, therefore, an ingenious device, *which takes from the landlord without giving to the tenant, and whilst ostensibly conferring a benefit on the cultivator of the land, really robs him of his capital as long as he has any land to cultivate.*

The third assertion requiring proof was that Tenant-Right maintained an antagonism of interests between landlord and tenant, which necessarily created uneasiness and suspicion. The old adage is probably applicable here, that the "bystander sees most of the game." When the writer studied this question *in situ*, thirty years ago, Ulster Tenant-Right had not assumed its present formidable proportions. In that interval it has widened its area; it has raised its terms, and is now striving to include within its range leases which were then entirely free from any claim of the kind, and other kinds of property besides land, such as mills, quarries, &c. There are also not wanting indications that no long time will elapse before a strenuous attempt will be made to establish *fixity of rent*. Even at present any considerable increase of rent on a large estate would probably bring on a struggle, the issue of which would be very doubtful. A case which came under the writer's notice last October, shows that not even the public advantage is allowed to prevail over the most extreme assertion of this unreasonable custom. An owner of a large property and large mills, employing a couple of thousand hands, wished to build more houses for some of his "employés," and for this purpose gave notice to quit to a tenant-at-will holding about 12 acres of land. The tenant did not reside on the land nor sufficiently near it to suffer any residential injury from its loss. The rent was 1*l*. per acre, and the tenant-right offered by the landlord 25*l*. *per acre*, which was more than double what had been paid for the tenant-right of the same land a few years before. The relations and the Roman Catholic priest united their endeavours to pursuade the tenant to give way, but in vain, and the building of the houses, which would have been a benefit to the whole neighbourhood, has been stopped by this unreasonable refusal of compensation exceeding the fee-simple value of the land. The landlord and his agent are kindhearted men, who do not like to proceed to legal extremities, though neither of them thinks that the threatening letters received would really be carried into effect. In 1839 such a case would have been simply impossible. Yet in the face of this steady advance, Ulster men, in general, do not seem to be aware whither all this is tending, and many of them maintain that if tenant-right were legalized its most objectionable features would be removed. Doubtless the evil consequences which flow from habitually setting law at defiance would disappear if the custom itself were made law, but the vicious principle embodied in the very nature of the transaction would come out more strongly than before.

The custom could be legalized in various ways. The new law might declare that the average of the sales within a certain district during the last five or ten years should rule the number of years' purchase to be given in future within that district; but, however small the district, it would be impossible to avoid injustice. Some men, who had given extravagantly high rates, would be great losers. How would it be possible to include in a general average such a case as the following? In March, 1866, MacB—— of K—— sold the tenant-right of a holding of about 4 acres of poor land, yearly rent 4s. 4d., for 45l., a sum equal to 207 years' purchase! In this district, if even the high average of 20 years' purchase were adopted, MacB.'s successor, on reselling his goodwill, would lose 40*l*., 13*s*. 4*d*. out of the 45*l*. paid. On the other hand, men in the same district who had never paid anything for tenant-right would have a present made them of a large sum of money for which no consideration had ever been given. A holder of a farm at 50*l*. rent would receive, at 20 years' purchase, 1000*l*.; and as it is notorious that the goodwill of the smallest holdings always sells at the highest rate, any fixed average would *give money to the rich farmer* and *take it from the poor one.*

Another method would be to charge the land with the repayment of the sum actually proved to have been paid by the incoming tenant for goodwill. This sounds easy; but numerous instances could be given of 30 and even 40 years' purchase having been paid for tenant-right, where the fee-simple of the land is not worth more than 20 years' purchase, and is already charged with mortgages and family settlements. If the landowner were made responsible for the tenant-right in cases like these, the property would have to be sold and the proceeds shared amongst the claimants; but, as they would be insufficient to satisfy the demands in full, who would have the priority,—the *former encumbrancers*, or the *tenant-right owners?* Neither of these two methods sounds very promising.

A third method would be to give every tenant-at-will a statutable right to sell his goodwill for what he could get. This method would be free from the complications of the two previous plans; but is the most vicious in principle of the three, as it would create two permanent antagonists on every farm. The *landlord* owning the rent, which, if raised high enough, would extinguish tenant-right altogether,. and the *tenant* having a legal claim to as much as he could get for his goodwill, but as the law would not help him to keep up its market price, he would, of course, do as he has hitherto done, *help himself*. And this very original plan for pacifying Ireland is to legalise the result already obtained by secret combination against the law, but to leave the tenant still defenceless against an unreasonable increase of rent; so that *fear, hope, and the consciousness of past success,*— some of the strongest motives which influence the human mind,—would unitedly urge the occupiers of land to renewed agitation in order to obtain Fixity of Rent. Many owners of large estates let far below their value, seeing that all is smooth on the surface, are difficult to persuade that there is an under-current of irresistible strength, moving slowly, it is true, but always in the same direction. Their tenants keep perfectly quiet, knowing their pecuniary advantages too well to endanger them by agitation; but they are keenly alive to the precariousness of their legal position, and should the present favourable opportunity for obtaining a settlement of the question be lost, no long time will elapse before a movement in favour of *Fixity of Rent* will arise in the North, which will assuredly fraternise with the demand for *Fixity of Tenure* in the South.

The opinions expressed in the foregoing pages on the general unsoundness and prejudicial tendency of Ulster Tenant-Right are substantially held by those leading men in Ulster who have taken the most pains to sift the subject thoroughly.

Lord Dufferin, in his able and exhaustive work,* which ought to be studied by every man who takes an interest in Ireland's social position, has expressed a very strong opinion adverse to Tenant-Right, and, in his evidence before a House of Commons Committee in 1864, mentioned that he had paid a sum exceeding 10,000*l.* in order to buy up and extinguish it on his estate. Lord Lifford, who has probably devoted as much of his time and personal attention to the improvement of the condition of his tenantry as any man in Ireland, and who resides in a wild part of Donegal where tenant-right prevails in its most unmitigated form, not only disapproves of the system, as carried far beyond compensation for the tenant's outlay, but, in a letter to the London 'Times' (Dec. 1869), stated that, after 30 years' practical acquaintance with Ulster Tenant-Right, he does not yet thoroughly comprehend it.

Captain Kennedy, in his Digest of the Evidence taken before the "Devon Commission" (published under the authority of the Commissioners in 1847),

---

* 'Irish Emigration and the Tenure of Land in Ireland.' 1867.

enters fully into the question of Ulster Tenant-Right. In his Introductory Chapter he speaks of it as

"A claim, not only made by improving tenants, but equally put forth by those who deteriorate the property entrusted to them. It is, therefore, in the great majority of cases, not a reimbursement of outlay incurred, or improvements effected on the land, but a mere life insurance or purchase of immunity from outrage. Hence, the practice is more accurately and significantly termed, selling the goodwill.* . . . . .

"Landowners do not appear aware of the peril which thus threatens their property, and which must increase every day that they defer to establish the rights of the tenant on a definite and equitable footing. They do not perceive that the present tenant-right of Ulster is an *embryo* copyhold, which must decline in value to the proprietor in proportion as the practice becomes confirmed, because the sum required by the outgoing tenant must regulate ultimately the balance of gross produce which will be left to meet the payment of rent.† . . . . .

"It is even questionable whether this growing practice of tenant-right, which would, at the first view, appear to be a valuable assumption on the part of the tenant, be so in reality; as it gives to him, without any exertion on his own part, an apparent property or security, by means of which he is enabled to incur future incumbrance in order to avoid present inconvenience — a practice which frequently terminates in the utter destitution of his family and in the sale of his farm, when the debts thus created at usurious interest amount to what its sale would produce. . . . . .

"The proprietor imagines, erroneously, that he has some advantage from this practice, as the principle observed in

---

* Digest,—Introductory Chapter, p. 2. † Ibid. pp. 2, 3.
‡ Ibid. p. 4.

such cases, when an arrear exists on the farm, is, that the arrear should be paid up to the landlord out of the purchase-money. It is true that he gets a settlement of the old rent account; but, on the other hand, he brings an embarrassed man into his land who is incapable of doing it justice, but well qualified to let a new arrear of rent accumulate! All parties, in fact, are sufferers!"*

After expressing so strong an opinion of the dangerous tendency of Ulster Tenant-Right, and of the inexpediency of legalising it in its present form, the writer will naturally be expected to propose his own remedy. It is simply to leave it untouched by legal enactment, but to place side by side with it the plan already proposed for the other Provinces; so that all occupiers paying less than 50*l.* rent would, on giving up their farms or being dispossessed, be legally entitled to claim five years' rent, in addition to remuneration for improvements on the basis previously explained.

The principal merits of this arrangement would be,—1st. That it would put an end, at once and for ever, to the antagonism between Rent and Tenant-Right. The payment here recommended is based on what is fairly due to a cultivator of the soil holding at will; but in Ulster it would at present, and probably for many years to come, be regarded as a payment for "tenant-right" or "goodwill." If, then, the legal payment for the so-called goodwill were fixed at five years' rent, a rise of rent would no

---

* Digest,—Introductory Chapter, p. 5.

longer encroach on the goodwill, but would *increase the amount of compensation to be paid to the tenant*, and rent would be restored to its proper position, as a matter of arrangement between landlord and tenant, having reference solely to the agricultural value of the land. The landlords would also be freed from what Captain Kennedy rightly terms "*the peril which threatens their property.*"

2ndly. The outgoing tenant, who is at present harrassed by uncertainty as to the future value of his tenant-right, would know that he could legally claim five years' rent in addition to the actual value of the buildings erected by him, and the unexhausted interest in his agricultural improvements, for none of which has he any legal claim at present. Should he have paid a sum exceeding this amount, it would still be open to him to abandon his legal claim, and sell his goodwill on sufferance, as before, for what he could get for it, though undoubtedly his chance of finding a purchaser at an extravagant rate would be greatly diminished by the alteration of the law, and as time went on would probably disappear altogether.

3rdly. The incoming tenant, who now frequently pays an unreasonably large sum for goodwill, which he can never be sure of recovering in full, would rarely be called upon to pay more than the legal five years' purchase, which he would be sure of being repaid on leaving, unless by his own default; and though even this sum is a tax which should not be thrown upon an entering tenant, he would receive some compensation by holding his land cheap, as rents can never rise to their fair value until landlords see their way to taking these payments upon themselves.

If such a plan as the foregoing were passed into law, the position of the occupier of land in Ulster would be materially improved,—an important consideration when endeavouring to estimate its chance of being favourably received. That there would be many dissentients is certain, whatever plan should be proposed, but those who would gain would far outnumber those who would lose. All would gain who hold land in those districts where tenant-right does not prevail, or where the current rate of purchase does not exceed five years' rent, and to these must be added a number of those who have paid more than five years' purchase, and who would yet be gainers by substituting a certainty of five years for a probability of more, especially when added to a legal claim to remuneration for improvements.

The suggestions indicated in the foregoing pages may be summarized as follows :—

Land Tenure.

1st. In the absence of any legal agreement for a longer term, tenancy to be assumed to be for five years, and, except as hereinafter mentioned, tenant to be entitled to five years' notice to quit, or six months' notice and a payment equal to five years' rent.

2nd. Tenants paying less than 10*l.* yearly rent shall, on giving peaceable possession of the land at the termination of the ordinary six months' notice, be entitled to a payment equal to five years' rent, less any arrears due, or any claim for wilful damage to landlord's property.

3rd. Tenants paying 10*l.*, but under 50*l.*, yearly rent, shall be entitled to exercise the option above mentioned, of claiming five years' notice or five years' rent.

4th. Where the rent exceeds 50*l.*, landlords to have the option of giving the five years' notice, or six months' notice and five years' rent.

N.B.—A payment by the incoming tenant with the landlord's sanction to be considered a payment by the landlord.

Tenant's Improvements.

On receiving notice to quit, or of increase of rent, or voluntarily giving up possession, tenant may claim the unexhausted value of improvements made by him or other members of his family or by a preceding tenant to whom he paid compensation. Tenant's improvements to be classified as follows :—

1. *Works not producing profit*, such as buildings, boundary walls or new roads absolutely required for the proper occupation of the land. Existing value of improvements of this class to be ascertained on change of tenant or increase of rent. Tenant to be entitled to the whole if erected solely at his cost; if jointly

with the landlord, present value to be divided in the ratio of original contributions.

2. *Works of a remunerative character*, such as drainage, reclamation of waste, &c. Twenty-one years' lease, or continuous occupation without increase of rent, to cancel all claim to remuneration for improvements of this class. Lease or continuous occupation for shorter term than twenty-one years, to cancel a portion of claim. Each year's enjoyment at original rent to cancel $\frac{1}{21}$st part of first cost of improvement.

3. *Prospective Improvements.*—Tenant may make all ordinary agricultural improvements without consent of landlord, but in the case of works of drainage or reclamation, the cost of which in any one case exceeds 50*l.*, and all works included in Class 1, tenant must give notice to landlord, who shall have option of doing the whole or a portion of the work himself, and charging 5 per cent. on his outlay. Landlord must intimate to tenant within six months whether he will proceed with the work himself or contribute a portion of the cost. If landlord object to proposed improvement, official valuer to be called in, who shall decide whether or no the improvement proposed by tenant is *unnecessary* or *disproportionate* to *value of holding.* If not, he shall give certificate to that effect, and tenant shall thereupon be entitled to proceed without consent of landlord. If landlord does not within six months intimate his approval or disapproval of works specified in original notice, his

consent shall be assumed, and tenant may proceed with improvement.

4. In order to ascertain the value of improvements, landlord and tenant shall each appoint a valuer, who shall, before commencing the valuation, agree upon an umpire to be called in, if required, whose decision shall be final. Failing agreement in the choice of an umpire, official valuer to be employed. Irish Government to appoint official valuers in each county or district.

Some people have imagined that it would be desirable to appoint Special Commissioners to hear and determine all cases of difference between landlord and tenant, even to the extent of determining in what cases a land-owner shall be restrained from exercising his power of eviction. It is difficult to perceive the advantage of such a course. If it were decided to adopt a plan somewhat similar to the one described above, the landlord's power of eviction would be clogged by the payment of a sum which would be an indemnity to the tenant for dispossession, and would act as so powerful a check to the exercise of the right of eviction as to prevent its occurring with sufficient frequency to cause any legitimate grievance; but it would not be necessary to appoint Special Commissioners to carry such a law into effect, as a valuer on each side, with an official umpire, would do the work in a much less costly and cumbersome way. The question whether the land-owner is to retain the control of his property, or whether it is to be transferred to the tenant by fixity of tenure, is one which must be decided by the legislature, and cannot be got rid of by appointing Commissioners to act as buffers between Parliament and the nation. Either the landlord *is* to retain the right of giving his tenant notice to quit, or he *is not*. If not, it would be highly unjust to the tenant that the Commissioners should confer such a power upon the land-owner at their will and pleasure; but if the land-owner is to retain this legal right, the Commissioners could not interfere to prevent its exercise, unless invested with power to set aside the law, or, in other words, to overrule the deliberate decision of Queen, Lords, and Commons.

The leading principle embodied in the foregoing scheme is that of giving to every occupier of land legal security for the capital embarked in his holding, whether that capital consist of money or labour; and, in order to simplify the question, the tenant's outlay has been classified under the three heads of:—1st. Ordinary farming expenditure. 2nd. Remunerative improvements. 3rd. Improvements that are necessary, but unproductive. The lamentable deficiency of the existing law on this subject has undoubtedly been the original cause of the agrarian outrages which have disgraced Ireland and humiliated England for well nigh two hundred years. It was universally felt by the cultivators of the soil that their toil and self-denial had created a valuable property, of which, on the plainest principles of justice, they ought not to be deprived without compensation. But the law was against them, and, as they were not strong enough openly to defy the law, they resorted to secret combination and conspiracy. These illicit proceedings resulted in the establishment of tenant-right in some counties and agrarian outrage in others. That the sale of tenant-right is greatly preferable to a state of chronic panic and occasional violence is undoubted, and Ulster Tenant-Right has done good service in its day; but so may a go-cart have propped the tottering steps of an infant, and to legalise the Ulster usage in its present form would be as reasonable as to padlock the go-cart round the neck of the grown man, and thus perpetuate the memory of his former feebleness and permanently impede his future powers of locomotion.

One of the difficulties of devising a scheme applicable to the whole of Ireland arises from the wide difference in the means and position of those included under the term holders of land. No three countries in Europe could be selected in which the condition of the occupiers of land differs more widely than the snug small farmer in the best parts of Ulster differs from the poverty-stricken cottier of the western coast, or than both do from the wealthy capitalist who pays some thousands per annum for a grazing farm in the midland counties. The writer has endeavoured to adapt his scheme to these striking differences by varying the course to be adopted towards occupiers paying certain gradations of rent.

Another difficulty is to find out any plan which will be acceptable to both landlord and tenant; and yet it is very plain that no change of the law can be successful unless it commends itself to the judgment of the moderate men of both these important classes. There are unmistakeable signs that neither England nor Ireland is in a humour to trifle with this question, and the land laws of the latter country will assuredly be sifted to the foundation during the coming Session of Parliament. In reforming these laws, the landlords may fairly be asked to surrender their present legal right of appropriating their tenants' property. It is a power which they never ought to have had, and which at present they are unable to exercise. On the other hand, the tenants' best friends are those who counsel moderate measures. It is not surprising that, whilst still smarting under the injustice of a code which leaves their property defenceless, the occupiers of land should rush to the opposite extreme, and demand "Fixity of Tenure;" but moderate men of all classes, though anxious to alter the laws which unjustly affect the rights of the tenant, will be slow to support a measure which equally unjustly ignores the rights of the landlord. The scheme proposed above is, it is believed, equally careful of the real rights of both classes.

When the writer commenced the foregoing pages, he anticipated being able to offer a few suggestions respecting measures which seemed desirable, in order to afford free scope for the development of Ireland's industrial energies and resources. One of the most important of these related to the consolidation and extension of her railroad system. The consideration of the land question has, however, occupied so much time and space, that the conviction has been reluctantly arrived at that further delay is inadmissible, and that the suggestions in question must be reserved for (possibly) some other opportunity.

Fortune-telling is not in favour with the present generation, nor is the writer conscious of any prophetic powers; but, having for some months had his attention concentrated on the varied evidences observable throughout the country of substantial progress accomplished during a period of many difficulties and much suffering, he cannot forbear from predicting that there is a good time coming, and that the next few years will witness an unexampled development of the latent resources both of the land and of the people. The unused capabilities of the soil are still so great that the country might double its yield of corn without diminishing its production of meat, and it may reasonably be hoped that the disposition to indulge in Repeal vagaries or Fenian follies will diminish as the serious business of the nation increases.

One last suggestion the writer ventures to offer, in all sincerity and earnestness. It is, that the sons of Erin should with one consent resolve to turn their backs upon the dark features of their past history, and with their accustomed energy devote themselves to working out a glorious future for the Rose, Shamrock, and Thistle. England will furnish solidity, Scotland constancy and perseverance, but the Irish element will be required to supply the brilliancy which will make the confederacy complete and irresistible. Without changing their ancient banner, or discarding their favourite motto, let them but inscribe above "Erin go bragh" the noble word "EXCELSIOR."

www.ingramcontent.com/pod-product-compliance
Lightning Source LLC
Chambersburg PA
CBHW022142160426
43197CB00009B/1393